Music, In A
Foreign Language

Music, In A
Foreign Language

Picador USA
New York

Picador® is a U.S. registered trademark and is used by
St. Martin's Press under license from Pan Books Limited.

Library of Congress Cataloging-in-Publication Data

Crumey, Andrew
    Music, in a foreign language / by Andrew Crumey.
        p.   cm.
    ISBN 0-312-14688-4
    I. Title.
PR6053.R76M87   1996
823'.914—dc20   96-24141
                                                    CIP

First published in Great Britain by Dedalus Limited

First Picador USA Edition: November 1996

10   9   8   7   6   5   4   3   2   1

C

The translation of C. P. Cavafy's poem NA MEINI on page 161 is by Mary Argyraki

Music, In A
Foreign Language

0

She was asking me (as was usual at such moments) what I was thinking about. So that I quickly had to make up some suitable reply.

In fact I was thinking of two things. First, of that spectacular diversity which leads every woman to respond to the moment of sexual climax in a unique way. There are those who shout, or gasp, or groan. Those who bay like wolves beneath a silver moon, or sigh with the heartfelt passion of a diva. Some who laugh, as if they had only just got the joke, while others shed a tear of misplaced sorrow. Women who collapse in satisfied exhaustion, and others who get up in a state of restlessness and make a sandwich, switch on the television. Phone their mothers.

But she, throughout all those years we shared, maintained with total consistency that low growling, like a half-sleeping cat disturbed. And afterwards, if she did not fall asleep, she would puncture the silence by asking me that dreaded question: What are you thinking? Which would always send me scurrying in search of an appropriate answer, since I knew from experience that honesty was not what was required of me at such a time.

I told her I was thinking 'nothing'.

This was not completely untrue; the path of my mental activity at that moment really was of no consequence, and could honestly be summed up in the dismissive manner I chose. But this nothing led – through no will of my own – to something. It had begun with her feline growling – the completion of the act we had just enjoyed. I now wanted only to have peace and quiet and a good night's rest (I had – if I remember correctly – to catch the train earlier than usual the next day), but instead my thoughts were prodded into action by her refusal to let the business end. I found myself imagining those other women I had slept with, or thought of sleeping with – and all those countless women with whom I would never have the pleasure of broadening my knowledge of life's rich diversity. I thought of that awesome variety, and I thought how strange it was that events should have brought the two of us together, so that I should listen to her cat-like purr, when I could equally well (had history gone otherwise) have found myself in the arms of a creature as different from my wife as a Chopin waltz is from a Bach fugue.

I mean this as no disrespect to the woman whom I now miss so much. But how could I confess to her then the speculations I was allowing – in a spirit of objective enquiry – into the alternative scenes which I might at that moment have found myself playing, if a thousand coincidences had been replaced by a thousand other equally probable ones?

My second thought was just as impossible to confess at the delicate moment my wife had chosen – for it concerned my need to relieve the bladder upon which she had not long before put much of her weight. I decided to bide my time. I told her I was thinking 'nothing'.

Of course, one can truly be thinking nothing only if one is dead. Even in my most idle moments, taking the daily train journey to and from work, without a book or sheaf of writing paper to accompany me (until today), still my brain is filled with thoughts which, because they go unregistered, are regarded as having no existence. I gaze out of the window; I see the sunshine on brown earth, and olive trees, and if anyone asked me I would tell them I was thinking 'nothing'. What a world of thoughts, impressions and sensations is thereby dismissed!

When I was sure she wasn't going to ask me anything else, I went to the toilet.

All of this seems very clear now in my mind, as I prepare to write the novel which first suggested itself while I stood barefoot on the cold floor of the bathroom ten years ago. Can my memory really be so accurate and vivid? There is of course the possibility that this memory – along with the story I intend to unroll like a carpet before you – is a pure invention, or at least a confabulation; an accretion of successive imperfect rememberings. Can I be sure that the need to go to the toilet coincided with a vision of the orgasm in its infinite variety? Or that this was indeed the night when Duncan and Giovanna first entered my imagination? Perhaps these events actually occurred on separate occasions, after distinct instances of love making. However, since that act, after a very short time during the first year we were together, soon became indistinguishable from one time to the next, it is impossible to conclude the matter with any degree of certainty.

Memory is, after all, far more than the simple replaying of the past. How can one remember, for instance, what it is like to see someone for the first time, when the image of them which you create in your mind is that of a face you have seen on a thousand occasions? Or how to remember a face seen only once? The image constantly amended with each successive act of recollection, until what is left bears little relation to what was originally seen. Whatever it really is (and I have often wondered), memory is not merely some kind of neurological video recorder.

But it was while in the bathroom, I feel sure of it, that the first manifestation took place of the story I hope now to write (if I am not disturbed too much from my work by the usual distractions which this daily journey offers me). Why should the idea have chosen that particular moment? Had it already perhaps been lurking incognito for a much longer time – for at least another ten years previously? I realized immediately that it must surely have been so.

Memories have their own vocabulary of associations and prompts. Often, while urinating, I am reminded of an unfortunate incident which took place when I was very young. In my haste to zip up my trousers after using the toilet, I managed to catch a very sensitive piece of skin between the two rows of teeth. Trying to pull the fastener back down so as to release myself only made the pain worse, and I cried out for help. My father came, and struggled with the zipper – making me yelp like a dog – but still to no avail. With his usual Biblical authority he said that this was the reason why button flies (such as he always wore) were far superior. None of which was of any help to me. Eventually, however, through the judicious use of some margarine, I was saved. Afterwards, my father laughed and said that if the operation had gone wrong I would have come out Jewish. Throughout half a century of living and peeing, the memory of that painful experience has come back to me time and again, whenever I am about to pull up my zip.

Fortunately, no such chain of memories intruded upon me on the night in question – the night which, I believe, was so crucial for everything that is to follow (since it was the night of this novel's conception) – for the simple reason that I did not put on my trousers when I left my wife to go to the bathroom. Had I done so, then I would no doubt have found myself thinking again about my father, and all the many ways in which I had failed him; and then Duncan and Giovanna, and Charles King and all the other characters who would begin to occupy my thoughts for the following ten years might never have been able to walk, unannounced, into my imagination. But no such urinary *madeleine* appeared to disrupt the flow of thoughts; instead some other impulse prompted my mind. Some random observation – of the cold bathroom perhaps, or of my own sensations, became combined with another memory – less distant, and together these produced the germ of the story which I have successfully put off writing until today. What prompt or stimulus might have led my mind in the direction which it took? Probably something which would otherwise have been completely insignificant; like when you find yourself humming a melody, and trace back your thoughts until you realize that the casual remark of another person, or a word you read, or some object, has been the origin of a chain of events culminating in a tune which you can't get out of your head. The novel I intend to write has felt rather like this. I say it all began that night as I stood in the bathroom, but this moment was itself a culmination of some other hidden process. But if I spend any more time thinking about it, then we can be sure it will be at least another ten years before I get anything done at all.

I relieved myself, and I did not suffer any sensations which might have carried me back to childhood memories of my father. But something made me think of a chance encounter long ago, and then I saw them, Duncan and Giovanna, meeting one day on a train. Where had these people come from? Where were they going? (Does anyone ever know where he has come from, or where he is going?)

My mind had now found a new association with which to torture me. Because whenever my wife and I now made love, I found that the act stimulated thoughts of these two mysterious people. They grew within me, resisting every effort I would make to suppress them. What are you thinking? my wife would ask, and I would have to dream up an appropriate lie, since really I was thinking about Giovanna, and whether she might be of the feline type or the lupine.

During the day, when I would get on with my paid work, it would be easy to forget all about those characters (teaching is such a wonderful way of making sustained mental activity quite impossible). It was during the nights that they would creep back – not every night, but frequently nevertheless. And whenever I saw them again, and the story which was beginning to encrust them, it always seemed slightly altered from the time before. Again, this might have been a trick of my imperfect memory. Or else they had begun – as writers always say – to 'take on a life of their own'.

But I was not happy with the thought of these foreign lives springing up in my head, especially when they caused me such trouble in giving an honest answer to my wife's customary post-coital interrogations. Because whenever she gave with a sigh that rhetorical question 'what are you thinking?', I was in fact thinking about how I might

11

appropriately begin a novel about fate, and the strange contortions of history; and it would be about two people who meet on a train, and the turn of events (wholly arbitrary, like all fiction) which has caused them to come together in this way. Even less chance then, of confessing to my wife the thoughts which were distracting me – she would ask who was this Giovanna, and why did I propose to write about her instead of my own wife, and then I should no doubt have been caught in the trap of discussing in too much detail a past which I had always presented to her in carefully selected highlights.

It was, I am sure, during that moment in the bathroom that the whole story began – or at least its first embryonic version. During the years to follow, it was a story which would be rewritten in my mind countless times. Had I chosen to begin setting it down a year ago, it would all have gone completely differently; Duncan would have discovered the truth he sought concerning that fatal car crash, and Charles King would have been forced to confess everything to the younger man. And if I were to wait another year, no doubt there would be other differences; perhaps Duncan and Giovanna would finally come together in an embrace which I now feel determined to deny them. If I were to record all the stories which those poor people have endured already in my head, I should need a dozen novels, not just one. But the time has come now for me to choose the one which will be committed to paper. How sad it is to have to make that choice, and bid a final farewell to all those alternative scenarios. Rather like the fond adieu you must make to a world full of women, when you at last decide on one with whom to spend the rest of your life. Had your choice been otherwise, who can know whether things would have been better or worse; one can only say that it would all have been different.

But of course, one can extend this reasoning into every aspect of one's life – by taking any particular course of action, one denies and loses for ever all the other paths along which one could have ventured. Sad, that life should

have to be a gradual pruning of that great tree of possibilities, until one is left with a single trunk, leading to a single
branch, and a single twig on the end of which one's life
reaches its ultimate conclusion.

And so I continued to dream of that other world in my
imagination, and I began to feel like the most abject and
faithless husband. When my wife would ask me what I
was thinking about, I would long to tell her the truth; that
I was thinking about how I ought to begin the novel I
would one day write, about a man and a woman who
meet on a train. And if I did tell her, then she would smile
and ask if she were that woman, and I should have to tell
her no, that it was another woman I was imagining, called
Giovanna. And then she would pout with dismay, and she
would berate me for my cruelty in talking about another
woman while I lay with her. She would be jealous and
hurt, and our life would be a misery until I promised to
cease thinking of the invented woman whose face and voice
refused to quit my mind. I knew I could never confess my
fantasies, and this only made them all the more stubborn in
their relentless growth, and sent their roots further into the
depths of my brain. I longed to be able to tell my wife
everything; to brave her wrath, or scorn, and perhaps even
persuade her to grow as interested as I myself was in the
thoughts which were my delight and constant burden. But
since I could never bring myself to discuss it with her, I
was never able to resolve the question of how to embark
on a story which I already saw in my head in a complete
yet inexpressible form. If only I could sort out the first
chapter, then surely everything else would naturally follow?
But in order to make that initial step, I would first have to
be able to overcome the sweet sense of guilt which coloured
my speculations. I would have to tell my wife everything.

And this in turn became a scene which I saw and
rewrote again and again – this confession to her of my
thoughts. It was a scene which grew in my mind in just the
same way as the story which it concerned. Once I could
get things right with her, then I would be able to put aside

all furtiveness, and set about fashioning the elusive first chapter. It was a problem which remained unresolved for ten years.

And it is only now – now that I am alone in the world – that I can see with sufficient clarity what the true opening should have been for this novel; an opening which denied itself to me for a decade but now emerges from the shadows of loneliness and sorrow, and presents itself to me like a new-born child.

A man is lying in bed with his wife; they have just made the most joyous act of love, and she asks him what he is thinking about. When he tells her, she does not frown or look annoyed. Nor does she express any displeasure when he says that he is thinking of the beginning of a novel – a novel which one day he will write and they will read together, the two of them, when they are old and past caring about life's difficulties. A novel about two people who meet on a train. She asks him excitedly to tell her about it, and so he says that it all begins with an image; the image of a motor car crashing through a barrier, and tumbling down a hill. And now she tells him that she would like to hear the rest of it.

1

It sounded no different from pushing an old, empty car
down over a hill in order to get rid of it; the speed at
which it had approached the bend, and the efforts of the
driver to save himself – if he had had time to make any –
did nothing to alter the impression that it was only
useless junk which was crashing heavily in the darkness
through low bushes. And the hillside was being littered
with the contents of a suitcase – socks, underwear, trousers
– and the contents of a briefcase also, or perhaps a file or
folder – papers were being scattered. All of this, they
would have to go over carefully afterwards. They would
gather every document they could find, for subsequent
inspection. Then they would take out the sheaf of typed
notes they had been given and throw them, a handful at a
time, into the air so that in the darkness the breeze would
catch them and they would fall naturally amongst the trail
of clothing, metal parts and other rubbish. And then they
would have gone back up to the roadside – how many of
them were there? Difficult to tell – two or three might be
enough. Perhaps one of them would have remembered to
check that the driver had not survived, or would not
survive. Perhaps they would have done him that final
service. Then back to the roadside – all quiet. The road
brushed clean of the fine black gravel at the bend; the
roadsign corrected – a row of chevrons, white on black,
pointing to the left; the metal board inverted and screwed
back in place – the chevrons pointing to the right. And on
the road itself, a black rubber solution easily removed with
industrial solvent – the word SLOW revealed in white
paint.

Had you been there to see it, you might have been
disappointed by the ordinariness – indeed, the banality of
the scene. The white Morris Commonwealth hitting the
barrier, the heavy crunching. All quite undramatic – not at

all like the films. Not in slow motion, but still ponderous and heavy, and not a good way to die. And all his things coming out of the door when it flew open, when it was pulled back on itself and crumpled under the body of the car then reappeared as the car turned again, the door flapping like an injury and the suitcase opening on impact. The briefcase opening on impact. The things, all those things left behind. The socks, the underwear, those trousers. The typewritten papers. The briefcase opening on impact. Or perhaps a file or a folder.

And when Duncan wasn't looking out of the window of the train he was reading a story by Alfredo Galli about a young man who sees a girl sitting in a bus and immediately falls in love with her. The bus is just pulling away from the stop as the man walks past. He sees the girl sitting near the back – she looks up and he feels he must speak to her. He tries to get on the bus before it picks up speed but the doors are already closing and the bus goes away with the beautiful girl looking round over her shoulder. So he remembers the number of the bus and every day for a month he rides this route as often as he can – his job as a cafe waiter permitting – but he never sees her. Then one night who should walk into the cafe where he works but the girl – alone – and she goes and sits in a corner and brings out a little book – like a diary – and she starts writing in it. And he is on his way to take her order when another waiter called Luigi – whom he hates – beats him to it and fetches her a vermouth and chats to her a little before he goes to serve another customer. And although he is desperate to catch her eye she only writes in the little notebook or occasionally stares out into space and he thinks she looks somehow sad 'like a nightingale which has lost its song.'

The train had reached the next station and Duncan became aware of people getting on – his solitude was threatened. Faces drifted past the window, peering inside, looking for spaces, and figures were moving down the aisle. Don't think now about the crash.

16

a nightingale which has lost its song. He went through his shift that night like an automaton; aware only of the girl in the corner of the cafe.

Someone had put a bag onto the seat opposite. Duncan glanced up and saw a girl with black hair – foreign looking. Now she was putting things up onto the luggage rack. She looked down at him – asked if the seat was free. Italian accent. He gave a nod, then she sat down and began to arrange some things on the table. A paper bag moist with sandwiches; a book.

The girl wrote with an air of concentrated absence, like a machine at work – though the steady movement of the pen resembled more some blind process of nature, which the young man watching found at once compelling and irritating – for the girl seemed wholly oblivious to everything around her; wholly uninterested.

Duncan heard a voice: 'I see you are reading Alfredo Galli.'

And across the pages of her book, the pen flicked like a mayfly.

Reading on a train is not like reading in the comfort of your home, where you can relax, stretch your legs, be alone. Be undisturbed, and break off only when you decide you want to. When you read on a train there are always other competing demands for your attention; stations appear and fill for a moment the little world of the window beside you, people come and steal parts of your space. They talk to you. And then other stories intrude on the one you are trying so hard to follow. The story you read on the train is a different one from when you are at home; it is a story full of interruptions, punctuations, digressions.

The Italian girl had been in Britain for a week. And now she was telling him why she didn't like London.

'At the Underground station – at King's Cross – I got robbed. The very first day I arrived here! Can you believe it? I was getting onto the train and there were some people pushing behind me to get on, and other ones were trying to get off, and I was in the middle like a little squashed beetle – I thought oh no, help – and then when I got on and the train started I realized after a while that my purse was gone! Not much in it, thank God – a few pounds only. But now I have learned to be more careful.'

The story you read on a train is a fragile, delicate thing; and though you look after it as best you can, still it can so easily become lost in the forest of other stories which you must journey through. She's not going to let you read, Duncan. Don't fight it. Her name is Giovanna.

Giovanna is brought up in Cremona, and spends her childhood longing for escape. She goes to Milan and is a student there, and many young men fall in love with her, and she falls in love with many men, but the ones who want her never coincide with the ones whom she wants, and she sometimes feels destined to grow into a lonely old woman dressed in black who sits at her balcony looking down on a world filled with regrets and unfulfilled longing. Or else she might compromise her high ideals and marry Fabio, who is sweet but tediously unrelenting in his efforts to please her. Fabio moves to Zurich, and every year for the rest of his life sends her a card on her name day.

She soon tires of university and quits her course, then finds work in a picture library, where she is hired because the boss wants to sleep with her, but he never succeeds, and she does her job well, finding appropriate photographic images to satisfy the requirements of the publishers, advertising agencies and other clients. For holiday brochures, there are photographs of Paris, Istanbul, Vienna and all the other great cities of the world. There is the Taj Mahal in full sunlight, or in the cool of the evening, or even a delayed exposure night shot with a full moon superimposed above.

Travel pictures are Giovanna's speciality. But then there are also the portraits of anonymous models, the photographs of every type of car, every type of salad. Photographs of new born babies, of corpses, of machinery. Giovanna grows tired of her job, and not only because of the occasional lecherous remark from her boss. In the room full of travel photographs, filed, labelled and cross-indexed like dead butterflies, she senses a world outside that is revolving without her.

But she told Duncan none of this, and when she got up to go to the toilet he was glad to return to his book.

The girl remained in the cafe for some time. She had another vermouth – which Luigi also brought. The young man watched the strange girl with growing fascination. He tried to compare her with his memory of when he had first seen her, sitting on the bus weeks before. He paid little attention to his own work – customers got the wrong change, or the wrong order. For more than an hour she sat in the corner, making her drink last. When she didn't write she would stare sadly at a point somewhere in space. Then, while Luigi was busy with a customer, she quickly got up and walked out.

'Hey!' The young man ran after her. The fact that she had not paid her bill was more convenient than necessary. She had gone out into the street – he followed. She ran, and he did too. The little book fell from her hand or her purse, and as he picked it up from the gutter and reverently wiped the dirt from the cover, the girl escaped from his sight and was gone.

2

Approaching the bend. Night. If you had been there you might have heard the dull pop of the gun. Not a shot 'ringing' out, like it always says in the books, but a sound like a small firework, or even a car tyre bursting; an unexciting sound, and the white car hitting the barrier, rolling and turning. Crashing down the hillside.

Duncan looked up and saw that Giovanna had come back, and he watched the curve of her hip as she slid behind the table and sat down again opposite him. Her hair seemed fuller now and freshly combed. She saw that he wanted to read, so she picked up her own book and the thick paperback fell open like a sliced fruit at the page she had marked.

At work in Milan, Giovanna makes a date with Franco, who runs errands and is three years younger than she. In her flat, she lies on the couch as Franco's inexperienced hands work clumsily on the buttons of her blouse, and she watches the silent flickering television screen. Then there is a news flash, tanks are moving in and out of searchlight beams and the red arcs of tracer bullets are finding windows, walls and people. She reaches for the remote control and Franco is annoyed, but too young and shy to complain, and she turns up the volume so as not to hear him. The announcer counts the people he has seen killed before him during the previous twenty minutes, when a peaceful demonstration turned into a riot. She sends Franco home, then cries for the people who have lost their lives, and for the life which she is wasting.

The ticket collector was coming down the carriage.

'Right. There you are love. Thank you sir.' The scrutiny of the ticket collector. 'Ah. You've got a blue saver here.'

'Yes,' said Duncan, 'it's a blue day today, isn't it?'

'No, white savers or standard fare today sir. I'm afraid you'll have to pay the difference.' The ticket collector

20

consulted the yellowed pages of his fare manual. 'That's another two pounds please.'

Duncan looked in his wallet and found a one pound note and another four shillings in change. 'I'm afraid I haven't got enough on me. I was sure Sunday was a blue day.'

'Not in Summer, sir.'

'But it's only April.'

'Well, Summer starts early here you know. If you haven't got it then I can take your details and you can send the money later. If you could just show me your identity card, I'll take your name and address.'

Giovanna interrupted: 'Duncan, please, how much do you need?'

'Oh, no, it's alright.'

'Please. What do you need? I have two pounds, look. Take it, please.'

'Well, how about if you lend me six bob and I can pay you back?'

When Duncan reached London on Friday he was carrying nine pounds and seven shillings. His fares, food and other expenses must have come to three pounds and three shillings. He had given five pounds to tip the man at the Office of Public Records. He would know to take more next time.

'It's very kind of you.' Duncan offered to send her the money, but she only laughed and told him to think nothing of it. And Duncan consoled himself with the thought that since she was a foreigner she could easily afford it.

For six months Giovanna does nothing. She continues to work at the picture library, has a few more dates with Franco, but tires of his company. Every day the television brings news of a world situation changing too rapidly for anyone to comprehend. Old ideologies are replaced by new ones, former enemies become allies. There is the changing of names – names of political parties, of government bodies, of countries. All of this happens on the television, and Giovanna's life seems trivial and insubstantial by comparison. There are the demonstrations in the streets;

the faces of the protestors – students, workers, artists. She is exhilarated by the prospect of revolution. She longs to go and be part of it all. But for more than a year Giovanna still does nothing.

Now they were both reading their books. Duncan eased his stiff legs back out into the space from which they had retreated, until he met the obstacle of her feet.

'Pardon.'

'Sorry.'

Reading on the train is not like reading in the park, when it's sunny and you can sit on a bench and stretch your legs and forget all your worries. Or on the grass; you can lie down and relax (after you checked for dog shit of course). You can lie on your side with the sunshine so bright on the page you have to screw up your eyes (it's always shiny bleached paper on the imports, not like the cardboard rubbish) – but that's not so good. It gets uncomfortable. Or on your back, with the book like a sunshade, and this is fine until your arms get stiff. Then you stop for a while and watch the girls go by in those tops they're all wearing now, and maybe one of them will look at you.

The girl's diary was dirty from where it had landed in the gutter. He wiped the cover, then waited in the street unsure of what to do. The girl had gone, so he went back to the cafe. Luigi was laughing. 'When you chase a customer for the price of two vermouths then you are certainly in love! But don't waste your time. I've already made a date with her.'

Better to shut your eyes now Duncan, and pretend to be asleep.

The car approaching the bend. Your father's white Morris Commonwealth approaching the bend, and then some obstacle, hastily erected – a fallen tree, perhaps, or another car, sitting in the road in the dark, and your father's inattention; his preoccupation, and the attempt to stop in time – the white Morris Commonwealth hitting the barrier.

Duncan felt the muscles relaxing in his legs; he felt his knees gently falling from the position he had held them in. He saw the flicker of sunlight through his closed eyelids. And he felt the side of his knee reach a part of Giovanna's leg. Only the vaguest of sensations; probably only her loose jeans that he was touching, so that she hadn't noticed. But he left his leg there.

(In the park, you see a pretty girl walk by. You call out from where you are lying on the grass and ask her the time, and she calls back and walks on, and you feel rather foolish because your own wristwatch is plainly visible. Though it might have stopped, of course. In any case, what's the harm in being obvious? Sometimes they like that.)

With the rocking of the train, Duncan's leg was bumping softly against hers, though she wasn't moving away.

And if you could have been there, Duncan – if you could have been able to see it. Nearly twenty years ago – you were only a young child. Your father's white Morris Commonwealth hitting the barrier . . .

The rocking of his knee against the unmoving obstacle. Duncan could feel the material of his jeans giving with the slight pressure against her leg; a pattern of changing sensations as the material crumpled and moved, from which to infer the nature of her limb – its shape, texture and other qualities. From this point of contact, he could try to reconstruct the rest of her body.

Reading in the park is not as good as reading at home, where nothing can distract you. Why did you need to read in the park anyway, when by simply going there you had already found the escape you wanted? But reading in the park is not for escape; it's more an excuse, since you don't like sitting there with nothing else to occupy you – except watching the girls in those tops they're all wearing now. But back in the flat, then it was a good time to do some serious reading, when Charles and Joanna still hadn't come home to interrupt you, and you could make a cup of coffee and sit on the floor with your back against the sofa.

Because reading is so good for you, and there are all those books you want to get through if only you can find the time. Maybe if you ration out the hours somehow; set yourself a programme, so much per day.

Duncan's knee had been held in the same position against her leg for so long now that it was becoming quite stiff and numb, and the pattern of textures from which he had been trying to derive so much information was now becoming submerged by the messages from other muscles, begging him to move. He gave a sleepy sigh and rearranged his leg, his eyes still closed, though getting a little sore now – and red patterns like oriental carpets swirling on his closed eyelids. He opened his eyes for a moment, and saw that she was concentrating on her book. When he closed them again he let his legs relax once more into a new position, until again his knee found its goal.

But even when you were reading at home, you were still thinking about the pretty girl in the park, and how she looked round then walked on, and it was as if she didn't have a care in the world – because sunshine has that strange way of making everyone seem happier than perhaps they really are. And then, before you could get much further, Charles got back from the university and you ended up in that stupid argument.

Duncan opened his eyes, and when he glanced under the table he saw that his knee had actually been resting against the table leg. The conversation was resumed. She had been staying in Cambridge.

'Such a lovely town,' she said. 'All those beautiful old buildings.'

'Mostly reconstructed after the war.' Duncan told her he was born there, but his mother took him away to live in York when he was four, following the death of his father. 'It was a car crash.'

'Oh, I'm sorry. He must still have been quite young.'

'Thirty-two. I can show you a picture of him.'

Duncan shifted in his seat to reach the wallet from his trouser pocket, and he pulled out a small photograph in lurid colours, creased and cracking at the edges. Giovanna took it from him, and saw three people standing in front of a white car; two men with a woman between, in a cream coloured dress – not very flattering. And in front of her a small boy. The sky looks an unnatural and poorly developed blue – it was a sunny day. The two men smiling uneasily, the woman a little stern. Some trees, and to the side of the car a suggestion of flat open landscape beyond the road.

'Is this you? The little boy? Oh, you were very pretty! And this man here – is he your father?' She pointed to the taller of the men, who stands close beside the woman.

'No, the other one. That one you're pointing at is the chap whose flat I live in now – he's called Charles King. They were close friends.'

'What was your father called?'

'Robert. Robert Waters.'

'And who is the woman? Your mother? She looks a little sad. I can see you've got her eyes. You don't look so much like your father, though.'

'You think so? I reckon I look more like him than I do my mother. I've got his chin.' Duncan leaned closer to look at the photograph. 'This picture got taken only a few weeks before he died. That's the car he was in.'

'What a shame. He looks very clever.'

'He was. He was an historian.'

'And the one you live with now – what does he do?'

'Charles? He's a physicist. Lectures at the university. I suppose it was his wife Joanna who took the photograph.'

'I can see a bit of her shadow – look here; on the road, at the bottom. That's her head. She had the sun behind her.'

Had the sun behind her. Though it was not Joanna who took the photograph, but Jenny – a girlfriend whom Charles abandoned soon afterwards. And although Duncan had tried to find out the truth about his father's death – and had been to London to check the records, now that everything was open to the public – he had learned nothing new. He still didn't know about Jenny, or the affair, or the chain of fear and mistrust which had led his father's car through a barrier and down a long ravine, twenty years earlier. He still knew nothing – he was still little more than a child, in a creased photograph.

3

For another five months Giovanna does nothing. Her job bores her – Franco bores her. But she stays in the same job, and she still sees Franco, as if there's nothing better for her to do. She imagines herself an old woman dressed in black. And she tells Duncan none of this, as he quietly returns to his book.

The young waiter left the girl's diary unread until after he had finished his shift at the cafe and made his way quickly home. The first page began in mid-sentence, as if it were the continuation of another, earlier volume, and at first he could make little sense of what was written in the even, regular hand of the girl; the letters curled and gently sloping. Neat letters, elegant and aloof. Letters of blue ink, set down rapidly. Letters which suggest a sort of urgency, a sort of compulsion. Letters which hold implication, which invite examination. Letters which seem to promise the answer to some question and then begin to suggest the darkening of a thought, the casting of an idea like a shadow. Letters which seem to push towards the light, but then send their roots deeper. Letters which begin to enfold and seem at first warm but then a little cooler, which seem to be there and yet dissolve into something else, and the coalescing into words which are placed in blue ink upon the page – and the spaces between words, and the bridge between the seen and the unseen, between the known and the unknown and the connections, growing like the healing of a wound, like the clotting of blood or the callousing of worn skin; the conspiracy of words and the assembly into sentences which seem observed yet knowing. Sentences which seem meaningless and yet have the weight of another's guilt, and which bring neither a warning nor a threat but only the confirmation of something previously suspected, and gradually the forming of a pattern, a hierarchy, and the sense that each sentence, each word, each letter of blue ink is not an answer complete in itself but only an indication, a hint, a point where things meet, a point of confluence, of ramification, and each letter, curled and silent, bears witness to a crime and the idea of a crime, and an act of intrusion by someone who begins to feel involved, and who begins to sense the need for escape but has already gone too far; someone who watches me and thinks he is not seen.

I shall run from this cafe without paying, and he will follow me. I shall throw this book to the ground, and I shall escape. He will pick the diary from the gutter, wipe it clean. But he will not yet dare to look inside. He will go back to the cafe, where the other waiter – whom he hates – will laugh at him and tell him that he has already made a date. So he will carry the diary back to his apartment – a small apartment, the sort of apartment a bachelor lives in, the sort of apartment where a woman will occasionally spend the night and then clean the place for him next morning as an act of sympathy, because when she slept with him it was out of another sort of sympathy, because he's the sort of man who spends most of his time alone lost in daydreams, the sort of man who sees a woman on a bus and pretends to be in love with her when all he wants is to fuck her and if he managed this it would only interrupt his dream, his love of himself and the images which he makes for himself. So he will lie on his bed in his apartment and he will open the diary with a sense of reverence, imagining somehow that this invasion is motivated by respect, and as he continues the intrusion his excitement will turn into anger because little by little he will begin to feel enmeshed, implicated. He will begin to feel that he is not an unseen observer but is

himself observed, that he is not the controller of
events but is himself controlled; that he is no longer
the protagonist but is now a peripheral character who
has entered the story of another; of a girl who goes
into a cafe and makes a date with a waiter called
Luigi - who happens to be a Fascist - and arranges to
meet him next day, and she can tell that he doesn't
care too much how it goes except that if he doesn't
get a fuck out of it then he hopes it doesn't cost him
too much, because she can tell that Luigi is that kind
of man – the kind of man who likes a fuck more the
less effort it takes him to get it, because it flatters him
and he needs all the flattery he can get, and it suits the
girl's purpose because to her Luigi is really nothing
more than a name – an instruction in blue ink on
white paper, and it doesn't matter much to her
whether or not Luigi keeps the date, or what they do
together, because he and the girl are themselves arbitrary characters in a story which seems to suggest the
possibility of some resolution, of some answer, and
yet continues to deny this, and it's the sort of story
which you won't like if you believe that the world
makes any sense, if you're the sort of person who
wants a beginning and a middle and an end, the sort
of person who can see a girl on a bus and think she
hasn't seen you and then ride the same bus route for
weeks hoping that you'll see her again, all the while
inventing stories in your mind and weaving together
the possible middles and possible ends, but still you'll
follow Luigi tomorrow, hoping that he will lead you
back into the kind of story you want, you will follow
at a distance and you will watch him meet the girl
on a corner near the fountain, you will watch Luigi
slide his arm around her, which she will neither resist
nor encourage, and you will follow them both at a
distance, as the only desire you know is the desire
to intrude, and you will watch them go to a building
three blocks away where you will see her then bring

a key from her pocket, Luigi's arm still across her shoulder, and they will go inside while you stand in the street and watch and torture yourself with your dreams. And after a while she will come out of the building alone, she will look neither to one side nor the other, but she will walk swiftly away, and if you should be able to make your way inside the building she has left, what scene of horror might meet your eyes? And if you should follow the girl, what other story might she throw at your feet? And if you should catch the girl and discover everything that can be known about her, what profit would there be in that?

But now it is late and you are alone and you know that what you took for love was only a kind of emptiness and what you took for a cafe was only another kind of emptiness and what you take for the emptiness of your flat is only another point in the same vast emptiness, vast and unending, and tomorrow maybe Luigi will die, and perhaps he deserves this, or tomorrow perhaps I will die, or perhaps it will be you, and you will close the book which you took to be a diary and you will go to the open window and look down on the street and although it is full of slow traffic and people mixing like fish in a slow stream, still it will seem to you to be another part of that limitless emptiness, and the narrow street and the people and the traffic will look like a line of letters on a page; letters which move slowly and yet go nowhere; letters which long to connect yet remain alone, letters which form meaningless words without beginning, middle or end. Some are the oppressors, others are the oppressed. Some the hunters, others the hunted.

Again her flat; the television on while the stubble of Franco's young face moves across her belly, and again there's the news – again the silent faces of protestors;

students in old-fashioned coats, and everything looking grey and dirty but Giovanna closes her eyes while Franco's stubble still blindly follows the paths of her skin. Only later does she tell him of her dream; to travel – to go and see everything for herself, and to feel a part of history, and his incomprehension only makes her more determined that this is what she must do.

The rain, falling at an angle with the wind. Car beams in the fine drizzle. Cones of white. Approaching the bend.

Next day her boss knowingly asks her why she looks so tired and happy, and she says she wants to take the three weeks leave that's due to her as soon as possible. He puts up a struggle but only for the hell of it because business is slack and he can easily manage without her in the meantime, and when she suggests he gives her a fortnight plus one week unpaid he moans and shouts and then gives in and is satisfied that he's won the deal. Ten days later Giovanna is on a plane to England.

If you had been there Duncan, what scene might you have witnessed? Approaching the bend, headlights full beam. Cones of white in the drizzle. The briefcase on the back seat – no – on the front seat; never out of his sight. The fatal manuscript. Perhaps a folder. And if you could have been there, Duncan, what act might have saved him? And if he could have saved himself, what story might he have told?

Then she's in London – it's like all the photographs in the library, only more grey. And there are no demonstrations now, no riots. Now they're renaming everything, rewriting everything, and it's as if it never happened. And she realizes that the revolution might only be a return to an earlier state of things, which she and the spectacled students are too young to remember.

Across the road, an oil slick or some slippery substance and the car hitting the barrier, then overturning as it makes its way down the hill, rolling and bouncing – crashing heavily in the darkness, and the hillside littered now with the contents of a suitcase – the things, all his things left behind – and the briefcase thrown from the door when it flew open, and the door crumpled under the body of the car, and reappearing as the car turns again, and the briefcase bursting open and the papers flying into emptiness, into drizzle, into grey drizzle, and falling in the wind.

Giovanna approaches St. Paul's Cathedral, whose baroque outline reminds her of Italy. She gives some money to the beggar at the entrance, then goes inside, and she is surprised by the whiteness; the great empty whiteness of the walls, which seem almost totally without features, until here and there she notices parts of the original fabric and decoration which were saved and incorporated in the restoration. But the plainness makes it look more like a drawing – like an architect's plan, with thin lines and semicircles pencilled cleanly against the white. She goes and sits on one of the pews, where she can look up into the dome.

And if they hadn't stolen his papers, Duncan, if they hadn't destroyed his work, how might things otherwise have been?

And Giovanna looks up into the great emptiness of the dome and she thinks of the young students and the workers and the old people – all of them – taking hold of history and saying yes, now is the time and she thinks about how at every moment things can go one way or another, but sometimes there comes a point when you have to have courage and you have to act, since there will never be another chance.

But London is a disappointing and a depressing place for her; she is saddened by the poverty, and the crime, and in Cambridge once again she is in a make-believe world of buildings reconstructed since the war. On the platform of Peterborough station she watches the train for Leeds come in half an hour late. The windows move past her and she sees the bowed head of a young man who seems to look up and perhaps he sees her. She gets into the carriage and walks along the aisle until she comes to the place where he is sitting reading a book by Alfredo Galli. She sits down opposite him, and they begin a conversation.

4

'The rewriting of history is not a purely modern preoccupation. Indeed, one could argue that history itself is little more than an accumulation of alterations and amendments; the endless recreating of the past. We need only consider the subtlety of the immediate present, and the infinite malleability of our own perceptions, to realise that the past is a thing without substance, without meaning, unless it is interpreted. And to interpret is to rewrite.'

It is no accident that I chose Duncan to be reading a story by Alfredo Galli – the author of the preceding paragraph. The tale of the cafe waiter, I confess at once, was my own invention; my tribute to a writer I have always admired (though attentive readers may have noticed that the motif of the mysterious girl on the bus has its origin in the anecdote of Lucia and the engineer in *Il Furto*). However, this act of simultaneous plagiarism and distortion on my part would not, I think, have offended the Sicilian who once said that the evolutionary advantage offered by the acquisition of language lies in the ability to deceive.

But how are we to respond to the assertion that history is 'little more than an accumulation of alterations and amendments'? Does this not contradict our own experience; the certainty of our own memory?

I am reminded of the case of F., reported in Lowell's fascinating study *Minds and Memories*. F., a man in his thirties, was involved in an industrial accident which caused a blow to the head. For several days he was in a coma, and when he regained consciousness he asked to see his wife and children. In fact he was unmarried, but could give a detailed description to the doctors of his 'phantom family', including birthdays, memories of things they had all done together, and so on. Therapy for F. had to begin with the destruction of the alternative reality which his injured brain had spontaneously created. Was this an act of cruelty on the part of the well-intentioned psychologists who treated him?

For F., his own memory, the internal history of his own life, proved indeed to be 'a thing without substance'. And if a whole nation of people share the same fantasy, the same mythic past, then does this make it any more real, and any less of a fantasy?

I remember a photograph in the Museum of the Working People, which showed a meeting of the Cabinet in the fifties. One of the faces seemed somehow different from the rest – that of the young Vernon Shaw. He seemed paler than the others; look more closely and you could see that the shadows on his features did not correspond with those on the other faces. The neck met the shirt collar at a disconcerting angle. Clearly, the face was superimposed on the body of another – presumably Herbert Lindsay – the alteration so blatant as to be laughable. But now the Museum of the Working People has itself been erased; the exhibits dispersed or destroyed, the name of the building changed on the maps, along with that of the street on which it stands. The place is now an exhibition hall. The last I heard, a display of Lego models was attracting huge crowds.

Do I regret the demise of the museum? Of course not. Do I rejoice in Lego models? Of course not. Old fantasies have simply been supplanted by new ones. History has been subjected to a further set of amendments and alterations.

Perhaps it is not even necessary to rewrite; one need only discard. Is it of any enduring interest to know whether the man at the Cabinet table was in fact Lindsay, rather than Shaw? And if we can decide with certainty that this was indeed the case, how does this affect our attitude to an exhibition of Lego models?

Such a view of things, the 'Gallian' view, is of course not to everyone's taste. And Galli's writing, though I find it endlessly entertaining, leaves others cold. It is hardly surprising for example that Bachaud should have taken such exception to *The Optical Illusion Last Friday*; a novel which takes as its basic method the continual pointing out of inconsistencies within its own plot. For Bachaud the rationalist, Galli's apparent antirationalism is the symptom of a degeneration of cultural values; Galli's suicide the inevitable end of a talent marred by lack of discipline. How ironic, I always think, that Galli's academic training was in chemistry, while Bachaud's is in semiology.

And it was the spirit of anarchism which pervades every aspect of Galli's work, and which can be so endearing when it isn't downright irritating, which first attracted me when as a young man I discovered the delightful *Racconti Impossibili* – the set of 'impossible tales' in which a description of a chair, for example, can gradually turn into an account of all the people who have sat upon it, and of all the other chairs on which they sat, and so on, in an endless process of multiplication which Galli cuts short with a comment such as 'the rest is obvious'. What Galli offers us in his writing is an escape from the tyranny of logic. In literature, everything is contingent; everything can be otherwise. To anyone who had grown up in Britain during the grim decades which followed the war, this fact was very seductive. I came to realize the simple truth that in the world, also, everything could have been otherwise – and the way things are is such a special case as to be almost irrelevant, compared with the full range of how things might be. Why then does history choose one course as opposed to another? This is something I have often thought about, while observing the evolution of women's fashion.

In Milan, where I have taught for the last twenty years, one has ample opportunity to conduct research of this kind. My late wife would be constantly complaining about the swing of my head as we passed another interesting sight; a girl in some particularly striking outfit. And I would reassure her that I was only considering the nature of history.

Twenty years ago, I remember watching a girl in a

striking black and white outfit, her figure as thin as a pencil. She had a long white jacket with huge black discs for buttons. It was one of the first things I saw after I arrived, harassed and sweating at the train station in my thick grey suit, and it struck me that the girl's outfit made her look like some kind of circus clown. And I wondered if I had left one kind of circus and gone to another – though at the time, this new circus seemed far more appealing. That was twenty years ago. Ten years later, no woman would wear such an outfit as that of the pretty clown in the train station. What had happened in those intervening ten years? History had happened. Everyone had grown a little older; young girls had chosen to reject everything their mothers had told them, new styles had appeared and been preferred – why had they been preferred? Who knows; they were certainly no better than the old ones, only different. Another ten years on, and once again the clown can wear her costume with pride.

We can imagine a grand book; The History of Fashion. I'm sure such books exist already; the one that I imagine is big, heavy, glossy – the perfect 'coffee table' book. It shows the evolution of costume – European costume, of course, with perhaps the occasional nod to other cultures. First there are drawings of primitive looking people in animal skins; a piece of whimsy designed to give the book an appearance of comprehensiveness. As we turn the pages we see mediaeval women with fantastic pointed hats and tiny waists, and then the evolution of incredible hooped skirts. The bustle has its moment, and then is gone. Now we are in the early part of our own century, though still it is hard to imagine anyone ever wearing things such as these; it's like trying to picture dinosaurs crashing through ancient jungles. And so it goes on, each period up to the present day illustrated by its own style. But then the last page shows a hundred models in contemporary outfits, and beneath the picture runs a solemn caption: *In today's ever changing world, we are at last free to choose, from the vast range of styles available, the one which best reflects our own personality.*

Of course, a hundred years from now, the successor to our book will illustrate with a single model the 'style' of our age. And if we could show our book to the mediaeval woman in the pointed hat, she might be perplexed at the unrepresentative choice we have made from her own rich culture.

Is the history of nations any different from the history of fashion? An ideology emerges, it sweeps across nations; it kills millions. And then its moment is over. Like the dinosaurs, it has simply gone out of fashion.

Where does it come from, this unstoppable force of change? Do the women of the world slavishly follow the whims of a handful of dress designers, or are the success-ful designers simply those with an eye for the 'look' of the age? Can an ideology be imposed on a nation of unwilling, uncooperative innocents, or must it be a reflection of something – some twisted parody of the collective spirit?

And can one call a halt to the process? For forty years a nation puts itself into the deep freeze of Communism; history is declared to have ended. There is no change; from one year to the next we drive the same car, wear the same badly made clothes, read the same books – or different versions of the same books. Even the price of a pint of beer remains for thirty years at the same fixed level. Then suddenly the freezer door is opened and burning coals are being thrown inside. And suddenly we see that everything which we thought had meaning was in fact an illusion. We see that power and fear are things which come in many varieties, and some varieties can simply go out of fashion. Was this all an act of kindness on the part of those who shovel in the coals?

I think again of F., and the details which Lowell gives us from the two lives of that unfortunate man. In reality he was, as I mentioned, an industrial worker in his thirties. A single man, rather solitary, who had few friends. In the period after his awakening from the coma, he spoke lov-ingly of his wife Nancy, a woman who worked part time in a grocer's shop, and whom he had first met some fifteen years earlier at a dance – a meeting that occurred by one of those strange, happy coincidences, when he and a friend went there because the cinema was already full. After courting Nancy for several months, she agreed to marry him, and over the years they had a son and a daughter. All of this, the psychologists would have to disprove. They would have to persuade F. that there was no dance, no Nancy, no fifteen years of marriage. Which would be the greater horror; to be told that your wife and children were dead, or to be told that they had never existed?

And should we tell Duncan that his father was not, in fact, the heroic dissident whom he imagines him to be? Should we spare him the endless rewriting of that scene, in which he imagines his father to have been killed by the secret police? Should we even tell him that his father was not killed at all? But then, as Galli would have said, what profit would there be in that?

They took away the Museum of the Working People and all its exhibits. Not only the photographs of the politicians; there were all those union banners, and the uniformed mannequins in glass cases, and all those paintings of strong faced men and women meeting their production quotas, and there were all the different kinds of miners' helmets, and the display cases full of badges. But it was all an illusion; the banners, the badges, the glass cases. It was all a mere photograph, cut out and superimposed on another mere photograph. And now there is an exhibition of Lego models.

For years, a nation lives in fear of itself, an imaginary economy is constructed in which debt and inefficiency is passed from one place to the next in an endless game – everything is decided by faceless committees in a way that is arbitrary, inexplicable, meaningless. The power, the ideology – these, it now seems, were all nothing more than illusions. Really, there was no power, no ideology; only fear. There is something of F. in us all.

But there is also a converse to F.; another case in Lowell's book. This is R., a woman suffering from severe amnesia, brought about by brain disease, which rendered her almost totally incapable of having any short-term memory. R. was cared for in the psychiatric hospital where Lowell worked. Every day, her husband would visit, bringing her a bunch of flowers, and whenever R. saw him arrive she would hug him frantically, telling him how much she had missed him and how terrible it had been without him. She would go through this scene every single day. As soon as her husband left, she would forget seeing him; all that would remain was her long-term memory of him from years before, and she would be filled again with sadness and longing. We have all known the experience of waking up and, for a moment, not knowing where we are – that feeling of disorientation, as if we have been suddenly put into a strange world. For R., every moment was like this.

Alongside the collective memory, the collective fantasy, there is also the collective will to forget; when once more the time has come for some 'alteration and amendment'. Not only was there no power, no ideology; not only was this all a terrible illusion, but it seems that it was the illusion of just a handful of men, somehow perpetrated on the rest of us. And now we are all filled with insatiable nostalgia for the time long ago, before their evil was allowed to pollute us. Again, there is something of R. in us all.

Why do these medical anecdotes fascinate me? For the same reason that Galli fascinates me; because I am reminded that what we regard as reality is only a point in an infinite space of possibilities. And everything we see has come about by an accumulation of accidents; the random preference for one possibility over another. Why have the banners and mannequins been replaced by Lego models? Why were the banners and mannequins there in the first place? There is no inevitability about any of it; we might as well argue about why the sun shines today when yesterday it was cloudy.

But I am digressing – so easy to let my mind wander, when I pause from writing and watch the landscape in its rich evening colours as it passes by the window of the train. Tomorrow I shall start again, and begin to tell the story of how it was that Robert Waters met his death.

PART TWO

5

Twenty years ago, when Charles King was still in his early thirties, he would leave his flat in Cambridge every weekend and take the train to London to be with Jenny.

They had met one afternoon while King was attending a conference at the Academy of Sciences. The lectures bored him, and so he went out onto the Mall to enjoy the sunshine. The street was quiet. On a corner, a policeman idly drummed his fingers upon his holster. It was August – the girls were in their summer clothes.

King loved women, or rather, he was fascinated by them. Watching a woman in the street, he would try to imagine how her unclothed body might look. For all his experience, this was still an unfathomable mystery for him. Although he could easily assess the volumes, the masses, the textures which ought in principle to lie beneath a cotton blouse, or a skirt; still that final act, that process of mental undressing, was a conceptual leap which forever lay beyond him. The naked image was an abstraction, a theory; a thing inferred, but not capable of being appreciated unless actually seen. This was something which intrigued him.

In the Mall, he watched the women he passed without questioning why he looked at them, or even asking what satisfaction it gave. He turned his head as a plant bends its stalk to the sun. In the case of the plant, the sunlight inhibits growth; the shaded side grows faster and the stalk bends. Perhaps there was something inhibiting too, in this preoccupation with the opposite sex; it was a thing from which he sometimes longed to be free. When he thought about it, he was aware of the irrationality, and yet also of the sober logic of his obsession. For all the metaphysical reasoning he might care to put forth, his response could be ascribed to the actions of various hormones, pheromones and other molecules. His behaviour was just as deterministic as the plant's, and just as irrational, if one attempted to embed the closed logic of chemistry in some higher meaning.

A girl was fiddling with a bicycle which she had placed upside down on the pavement while she dealt with the faulty gears. She was wearing a thin white top, which hung low as King approached and the girl's concentration remained fixed on the bicycle. He tried to reconstruct, from the fragment of cleavage that he could see, her breasts and the rest of her body. He stopped and asked if she needed any help with the bicycle. This was how his affair with Jenny began.

Every weekend, he would leave his flat in Cambridge and take the train to London to be with her.

Jenny was twenty-three. A few months before King stood in the Mall watching her as she mended her bicycle, and she watched the play of his eyes on her body, she had been rejected and left by the man she had been engaged to for over a year. She knew that the connection between love and happiness is a tenuous and uncertain one, and she soon knew that for King the connection between sex and love was equally arbitrary. Nevertheless, she was willing to join with him in the strange contract which he offered.

She found him good looking, though a little old (he was her senior by nearly ten years). She liked his shoulders, and his eyes. When he told her he was a physicist, she guessed he might be involved in nuclear secrets. This frightened her. But he explained that he was a theoretician; his only tools were pen and paper and his imagination, and then he seemed to her like some kind of exotic poet.

She gave him her address (there was no phone), and then she had to get back to work. Later that afternoon, he went to her flat.

When she undressed in front of him, she felt fearful and uneasy. She thought about the risk of getting pregnant. King told her to relax, and to remove her clothes slowly, as if her garments were so costly and special that she had to take the greatest care with them. While she did this, she

44

did not watch his face. When the last piece of her under-wear was removed it was, to King, like a narrow mask being drawn away so that suddenly the identity of the person beneath can be recognized. Her body, like her face, had to be seen in its entirety. When she got into bed with him, she was surprised that he did not want to have sex with her. They lay together, and then went to sleep. Afterwards, she felt she understood him less, but liked him more.

I said that King was fascinated by women. More precisely, he was intrigued by the differences between them, and the similarities. It was in the space between women that his real interest lay; this was the warm niche in which his fantasies lived. He noted the variations in temperament, character and anatomy; subtle yet so crucial, and as decisive as the difference between, say, a Gothic arch and a Baroque one.

Do I mean that he regarded women as cathedrals, of a sort? Not necessarily, but even so, women were a kind of religion for him. The act of desire was the one true act of faith which he knew.

That narrow void between the clothed and the naked, between one woman and another, between the potential and the actual; this was the world of King's fantasy. He was thrilled more by what could be than by what was.

Jenny's flat in Bayswater was small and claustrophobic; hardly more than a bedsit. Like everyone else, she was on the waiting list for anything better. When King first saw it, he was touched by the way she had tried to transform the place into a home in microcosm. This made him feel a sadness which took the edge from his sexual anticipation. It was like a miniature parody of domesticity, and it suddenly made him feel as if he were entering the play-house of a little schoolgirl, and then he felt terrified by the thought that he might want to use her body. It was a moment of disarousal.

The flat was really quite typical; a small sitting room with a bedroom (or rather, sleeping area) separated by a curtain. And a tiny kitchen, the sort that might have been designed for a canal barge. The bathroom was outside on the landing. Every so often, King would hear its door open and close, and he would hear the liquid drumming of a person urinating. Someone living here, he assumed, would begin not to notice these things.

Jenny went to the vestigial kitchen and lit the gas to make a pot of tea. This was the point around which they had negotiated his presence in the flat that afternoon. He told her to forget about that, to come back, and to take off her clothes. She did not know how to respond to this.

When he had first entered the flat, King noticed the vase of flowers on the mantelpiece, and the clean, patterned curtain which hid her bed. He noticed the photographs fixed on the wall, of her family and friends. And he imagined that he had entered the play-house of a little schoolgirl, and he felt horrified by this thought. He felt sordid and unaroused, and he tried to recapture the thrill of excitement he had known only a few hours before, when he had stood on the Mall and watched her breasts, and he had imagined what her naked body would look like, and how it would feel to run his tongue across the smooth flesh which he had glimpsed beneath her white top. But he could not recapture that sensation. Still he felt sordid and unaroused when she went to make a pot of tea, and he watched her body as she moved, and he tried to imagine the pleasure of her skin next to his, and still it was as if he were watching a defenceless child; a woman's body, but the soul of a little lost child, who misses her family and keeps photographs of them on the wall. He told her to come and take off her clothes.

She did not know how to respond to this. She realized that she had not yet asked herself why, precisely, she had invited this strange man to her flat. She had of course known that it might lead to them having sex, and she had been prepared simply to see how things went. But this was too abrupt. It seemed to break the rules. She switched off the gas and turned round to look at him.

'You,' she said, 'take yours off first!'

And so he undressed. And when he was finished, and stood naked before her – the first naked physicist she had ever seen (strange thought!), the first man she had met in a street and who had come into her flat and stripped for her – then she looked at his body and his shoulders, and his member was like a little flaccid fruit, nestled beneath the wiry shade of his pubic hair. He pulled back the curtain and lay down on her bed, which creaked like an old pram, and then she began to undress, nervously. He told her to relax, to slow down, and to imagine that her clothes were so rich and costly that she should take the greatest care with them; which puzzled her, and reminded her of a game she used to play when she was a little girl, and she would pretend to be a princess. Then she got into bed with him, and they lay naked together in silence.

Every weekend, King would leave his flat in Cambridge and take the train to London to be with her.

From the outset, he made it plain to her that his body was the only thing he was prepared to offer her, and hers was all that he asked for. He told her that he slept with other women, and that he loved none of them. Or all of them, since love was nothing more than a process involving the transport of certain ions across certain cell membranes. And he was not interested in chemistry.

All of this troubled her. It seemed to go against all the rules she had been taught, and all the other rules she had laid down for herself. Can love be reduced to a chemical reaction? But the fact was, that there was something exciting about the idea. She had had enough of demanding men, who had pretended to love her in order to sleep with her; who had loaded all the shit in their lives onto her, and who then had told her that she was the cause of all their problems. Love was a chemical reaction, and their bodies were nothing more than molecules to be experimented with. She still did not believe this, but the outer fringes of belief seemed tempting.

They lay together, naked, and they fell asleep. When she

47

woke up it was dark and quiet. She was lying with her face towards the wall. At her back, she could feel King's body, warm and hard.

When she had stood naked in front of him, his member was like a flaccid fruit. Now she felt him hard and asleep against her back. There was one chemical which said 'flaccid'; there was another which said 'erect'. They were like two jars on a shelf in a laboratory. When she stood naked before him, it was the jar marked 'flaccid' which was used in the experiment. Now he was asleep, and the other jar had been brought into use. It seemed a matter of chance which one should have been chosen.

She heard him give a heavy, sleep-laden sigh, and he moved his hand onto her hip. She began to feel herself becoming aroused. There was another shelf in the laboratory; two jars marked 'dry' and 'moist'.

When King woke up he turned her towards him and they copulated. He brought her to orgasm, and a tear ran down her cheek. Then he withdrew from her and pulled on her bathrobe which was hanging on the door, and he went out to the bathroom. The bathrobe was ridiculously small for him, and he was glad not to encounter anyone on the landing. He came back in and lit the gas, and began to make the tea they had abandoned earlier. She watched him, in the ill-fitting bathrobe, and she laughed.

Her laughter, and the tear that had run down her cheek, were of course simply further examples of King's chemical reactions. Feeling him deep inside her, her soul had tightened like a knot. She had seen images she would have preferred not to. She had thought of the risk of getting pregnant if he wasn't careful enough. And two more chemicals, marked 'pain' and 'pleasure' had been poured over her body. Her orgasm was like a chord pulled tight until it breaks. And a tear welled in her right eye, and trickled down her cheek; as if she had been thinking sad thoughts. And when she saw King standing over her gas ring, in her bathrobe, she laughed. The chord of anxiety was finally snapped. Her orgasm had shown her the possibility of pleasure without reference to anything. When she saw King making tea in her ill-fitting bathrobe, this became a reference point for her amusement. And when she laughed, it was the same tear which welled again in her eye.

He brought two mugs of tea, and when he sat on the bed it creaked beneath him. She sat up and took one of the mugs from him, and held it between her hands, sipping slowly and looking over the top of it at King, who was sitting on the edge of the bed and staring into the middle of the room, still wearing the ridiculous bathrobe. She asked him what was in his mind, and he told her he was thinking about something that had been said in one of the lectures at the conference. She asked him what his work was about, and he told her it concerned the fundamental forces between particles, and that really all interactions were just different versions of the same thing, but that their symmetry had been broken. He continued to look into the middle of the room.

She tried to understand what he was saying about interactions and forces. She imagined the forces of good and evil, of love and hate, of will and desire, and she tried to imagine how really they were all instances of the same thing.

And then she thought again about the orgasm, whose satisfaction she could still dimly feel inside her, and she wondered if in fact there was in her life only a single orgasm which she revisited again and again – a place which she had gone to by so many different routes.

At that moment of her orgasm, King was thinking about what had been said in one of the lectures. The thought had come to him quite involuntarily. He saw a calculation that would be worth trying to do later on. He would begin it on the train back to Cambridge. He thought about it while he lit the gas and made tea, and while he sat on the edge of the bed and gazed into the middle of the small room.

They both dressed. It was still early in the evening. He

was hungry, and suggested they go out and find somewhere to eat. She knew a cafe nearby. It was a cheap place where people were sitting singly or in pairs at the fixed tables projecting from the walls.

King ordered egg and chips, Jenny a sandwich, though even this proved too much for her. She had no appetite. Watching the pale runny yoke of the fried egg on King's plate, she felt a wave of nausea.

Afterwards, he walked her back to her flat, and then he said he ought to go, and that if she liked he would come and see her again next week. This was how his affair with Jenny began.

6

On the way back to Cambridge, Charles King began the calculation which had suggested itself to him while a tear ran down Jenny's cheek. The problem proved more subtle, more fruitful than he had suspected, and two months later he had finished writing a paper on it. During that time, he had continued to visit Jenny every weekend, to have sex on her creaking bed. For the rest of the week, King would forget about her completely.

He was pleased with his paper. He next had to get it typed before sending it for publication. He could leave it for one of the secretaries to do, but if he waited in line it might take weeks, and King was eager to send a copy of his work to the speaker he had heard at the conference; the one he had thought about while a tear welled in Jenny's right eye. So he first asked Doreen, with whom he was on good terms. Doreen was willing to put him ahead of the queue, but she had a lot of work to do for Professor Saunders, and she wasn't prepared to spend every hour of the day typing people's papers. So then he tried Joanna, who was new. She proved reluctant – perhaps afraid of setting some kind of precedent. Next morning he left on her desk a pair of nylon stockings which he'd bought while at a conference in Paris (he had a large supply for use on such occasions). Joanna angrily told him to wait his turn like everyone else. She didn't return the stockings.

King decided to do the job himself. He borrowed a typewriter from his friend Robert, then wrote to Jenny to explain why he couldn't see her that weekend. And he began to type the paper – a tedious job. He had little practice in typing, and had to look at every key he stabbed. For two days he struggled with the machine, correcting countless mistakes. He quickly grew to hate the paper which had so excited him when he was scribbling it all down in longhand, and the calculation which had suggested itself to his imagination during his first visit to Jenny's flat.

On Friday night the doorbell rang. It was Jenny – she had come to type his paper. He asked how she had known where to find him, and she pointed out that he had put his address at the top of the letter. She had asked for the street when she came out of the station. King was very careful about giving his phone number or his address to a woman. By including it in the letter, he decided, he must really have wanted her to come, like this. Her hair was wet – it was raining outside. He brought her in, took her wet coat and gave her a towel. He felt touched that she should have made this journey for him. He felt almost guilty. He tried to identify the reason why he was not glad to see her.

King's flat was quite unlike Jenny's. To her, it seemed luxurious. It was much larger, and she was impressed by the books which were packed onto every shelf. She was struck by the idea that she would like to live in the place where these books belonged. There was an old upright piano – she told him she wanted to hear him play, and he said that he would, tomorrow. And there seemed to be things from all over the world – a Russian samovar, and an absurd model of the Empire State Building, which was some kind of cigarette lighter. When she asked incredulously if he had been to America, he told her quite calmly that yes, he had. He spent three months doing research at Brookhaven, on Long Island. These names sounded to her like magical incantations.

He had got this flat as a prize. He came top in his final exams, and as well as being taken on as a Ph.D. student, he was allowed to rent the flat. And he had stayed here, while he had finished his Ph.D., and then had been appointed as post-doctoral associate, and then as junior lecturer. If he carried on up the scale, he would one day get an even bigger place.

She asked to see his paper, and this seemed like another kind of magic. Not only the mathematical symbols, but also the words were incomprehensible to her. She slowly read out a sentence:

We begin with the Lagrangian for a free massless fermion.

The words sounded strange on her lips, and for a moment she seemed to King like a little child, just learning to read. She pointed to the strange symbols and asked him how she was supposed to type those. He told her to ignore them, and he would write them in later.

Next day, she typed the paper. When she began, he was impressed by her speed, and accuracy. What had been so difficult for him, she now did easily. She asked him to play the piano while she worked. Anything, she said. He took the volume of Beethoven sonatas from the shelf and opened it at the Waldstein. She said she liked it, especially the slow bits. They spent most of the day like this; she on the typewriter and he on the piano. They were each alone and absorbed in what they were doing. Yet it somehow brought them closer.

It was strange having a woman in his flat for more than a night. She left her toothbrush in the bathroom, and a small washbag. He felt the miniature parody of domesticity spreading onto his territory. He almost expected a vase of flowers to appear.

On Sunday morning, Robert phoned to ask how things were going. King told him it was finished, and he could have his typewriter back. Robert said he'd come and collect it. King would have preferred to have gone to Robert's, but Robert had insisted; as if he were offering to do King a favour. He appeared at King's door not long afterwards.

When Robert came inside he was a little surprised to see a strange woman. Jenny shook his hand, and King introduced her as a friend from London.

King offered him a drink, but he said he was busy and he'd better not stay long. In the end, he settled for some coffee. King asked him about Anne, and their little boy. Robert said they were both fine, though Duncan had a bit of a cold. But Robert's mind seemed to be somewhere else. When he'd finished his coffee, he took the typewriter and left. After he was gone, Jenny asked if he was always so abrupt. Yes, King told her, he usually was.

53

Later, King took Jenny out for a walk. She asked to see where he worked, but he said it wasn't possible to go inside at weekends. They went back for dinner, which Jenny cooked, and then she pulled him to the floor where they made love.

Jenny said that she could stay until tomorrow morning if he liked; she could catch an early train and get to London in time for work. But he thought it better if she went back tonight. This upset her, though she didn't complain.

On the train, she wondered if this experiment was working in the way she would have liked. Perhaps she had been wrong to do all that typing for him. Next time he could bloody well do his own.

After she had left, King phoned Robert:

'It's alright, I'm alone now. Do you want to come round?'

Robert appeared at the door soon afterwards. King knew when he saw him earlier that he had wanted to talk, if Jenny hadn't been there. He brought him inside and took his coat, drew up an armchair for him and poured two glasses of brandy.

'So what's up? It's not Anne is it?'

'Anne? God no. She's fine.' Robert tipped his glass back and swallowed some brandy. Then he got up and went to the window, pulled back the curtain and looked out into the darkness. 'I can talk to you, Charles, can't I? It is safe to talk?'

'Well I don't think they've ever bothered to bug the place, Robert, if that's what you mean! Look, why don't you come and sit down and tell me what's going on?'

Robert went back to his chair. 'My office has been searched.'

'Searched? Are you sure?'

'I went there this morning to get some notes I'd left. I haven't been in for a few days − it could have happened some time during the week. Someone had been inside; things were moved around. Only slightly, but I could tell.'

'Did they steal anything?'

'No, there was some money in a drawer and they hadn't touched that.'

'What were they after, then?'

'I don't know.' He emptied his glass. 'How about another drop, Charles, there's a good chap?'

'Steady on there.' King passed him the bottle. 'It could all be perfectly harmless, of course. People walk in and out of my office all day as if it was St. Pancras Station. Are you sure it wasn't simply someone looking for a book?'

'No, Charles, they'd been in the drawers and filing cabinets.'

'In that case, I suppose the University authorities or the departmental spy decided to pay you a visit to keep a check on things – it's not so unusual. There was nothing for them to find, was there?'

'But it's frightening, Charles. If you're suspected of something it's halfway to being found guilty; you know that.'

'Even so, there was nothing they could actually get on you, was there?'

'I don't know.' Robert took another large sip of brandy, and got to his feet. He walked slowly to the window, deep in thought. Then he turned round and looked at Charles. 'This is strictly between you and me.'

'Of course.'

'A couple of months ago I was nominated to do the research for a book – history of revolution. It'll be an official text.'

'Then congratulations – I never knew you'd become an "official" historian.'

'The point is, Charles, it's a pretty sensitive job – I shouldn't be telling you about it. There'll be all sorts of archive material to go through – classified documents and so on. So I realized there would be a certain amount of vetting.'

'Should think so too. Don't want any damn progressives on this one, do they?'

'But I didn't think they'd do things like break into my office.'

'Well, maybe you'll just have to get used to it if you really want this job so much. Anyway, Robert, I'm sure they've already got a file on you as long as your arm. Discipline like yours is prime territory for subversives. But they've never given you any trouble before.'

'I know, Charles, I know. Why do you think I've always been so careful?' Robert returned to his seat.

'If you don't like being in the limelight, then maybe this book isn't the thing for you.'

'It's not as simple as that, Charles. The book is a really big project. It could be the best thing that's ever happened to me. It'll put me right at the top. And if I say no then I can forget about promotion or research grants. They don't like it when you turn down an offer you're not supposed to refuse.'

'But you could say that work pressure is already too great – I don't know – it can't be so hard to think up a valid excuse.'

'But Charles, the point is I want this job. You don't know how much I want it. Really. The trouble is, I also don't want them digging around in my life.'

'It's only the odd poke, though, by the sound of it. And what is there for them to dig up? You're always so discreet.'

'What if they find out about Flood?'

'Flood?' Charles laughed. 'Come on Robert, that was a long time ago. Must be five years at least.'

'It could still be very awkward.'

'Oh Robert, really. A little youthful indiscretion.'

'You may call it that, Charles, but it's a bit harder for me.'

'It was all so tame, Robert. I'm sure it only ever got read by half a dozen people. And in any case, even if they were to come up with a copy, if one still exists – how are they supposed to know it was you who wrote that stuff?'

'Yes, yes, I know. But Charles, I've been thinking. They'll probably interview people; family, friends, colleagues. They might want to talk to you.'

'Fine. I'll tell them what a splendid Communist you are.'

'Look, I know I can trust you Charles. It was just if they asked things like how long you'd known me, and how we met and so on.'

'Robert, I'm not stupid. I'm hardly likely to tell them about Flood. Anything that might implicate you would look just as bad for me.'

'Of course. My point is – it would be easy . . . You might say something about me that could compromise me in some way; it might not sound good.'

'Do you think I'm going to tell them you're a homo-sexual?'

'No, but they'll ask questions, and they'll make infer-ences. And you're the one person they're likely to interview who would be in a position to let something slip.'

'Well, rest assured, I won't be letting anything "slip". Is this why you're so worried about them breaking into your office?'

'I've been thinking about it all day, Charles. You were the only one I could talk to. I've been trying to remember if there was anything – a telephone number, or a note in a drawer. It's so easy to forget things like that.'

'But even if they did find out; would it be so terrible? Half of Cambridge is queer, and nobody gives a damn.'

'This is a Government job, Charles, classified. They don't want any security risks. And losing the contract would be bad enough, but suppose they decided to give me a hard time? You know, set an example – keep up morale and all that. I could find myself facing five years for immorality. I could lose my marriage, my career, everything.'

'Is this job really worth all the risk if there's so much at stake?'

'It's too late now to do much about it. They've already started digging around. If everything works then it's the best thing ever, really. I've only got to make sure that nothing goes wrong. The chances are very slim, but I had to see you, Charles. And when they talk to you . . .'

'Of course. And as for searching your office; even if they got hold of a phone number, he'd simply say he was a friend, wouldn't he? He'd have his own skin to look after. Look, Robert, relax – you should be celebrating. Big honour like this. Somebody on high must like you. Why don't we have some more of this cognac; good stuff, isn't it? I brought it back from my last trip to Paris.' King refilled their two glasses. The alcohol was making Robert calmer.

'Thanks, Charles. I feel such a fool, really. Coming round here in a panic like that.'

'It's not very pleasant to have them spying on you. But it's happening all the time; it's only alarming because you know they're there.'

Robert raised his glass again to his lips. He was beginning to look flushed and slightly drunk. 'Who was the girl?'

'Jenny? I told you, a friend of mine from London.'

'What does she do?'

'Some kind of clerical job.'

'Is it civil service?'

'She's with the Electricity Board. Don't worry, she's not a spy!'

'How do you know?'

'Well, I don't know. But she wouldn't be able to tell them much, even if she was.'

'You didn't tell her anything about me, did you?'

'Of course not. She said you were a bit abrupt, though.'

'Abrupt?'

'She could tell you were nervous about something.'

'What else did she say?'

'Nothing. I told her you're always an awkward bastard, which you are, and she didn't mention the matter again. Please, Robert, don't get so paranoid. Just because somebody has a sniff around in your office, you think the whole world's watching you.'

'All the same, don't say anything to Jenny, or anyone. This is all strictly between the two of us.'

'Yes, of course Robert. You know, with your suspicious mind you ought to be working for them, you'd be ideal.'

Robert drank the last of his brandy. 'I'd better be going.' He stood up and handed the empty glass to King. 'Thanks for listening, Charles. I don't like to rush away, but I didn't want to leave Anne on her own. Duncan's got a cold and she's got her hands full looking after him.'

'He's a lovely boy. You're very lucky, Robert.'

'I know. I sometimes forget it. You should get yourself a wife, Charles.'

'I'll bear it in mind.' He put the glasses on the table and fetched Robert's coat. Then he saw Robert to the door and wished him goodnight.

King went back inside and took the empty glasses to the kitchen, where he washed them in the sink. He returned to the sitting room, still thinking about Robert. Flood was nothing. Only two fools who thought that intellectual argument could have some effect on the world.

On his desk, the paper lay neatly typed. He still needed to write in all the equations, but he didn't want to start doing that tonight. It was late, and he could feel the brandy in his head. He went to the bathroom and brushed his teeth. Perhaps they would come and interview him. He would say nothing. Could Robert ever have believed otherwise?

Jenny had left her toothbrush, and a small washbag. He picked up the bag and opened it. There was a bottle of shampoo, and some soap. A flannel, a piece of sponge. A jar of something. Perhaps he should have let her stay. Next week he would take her a present. She'd like that.

7

On Monday morning, Charles put the pages of his paper in a large manilla envelope, along with the carbon copy Jenny had made, and went to his office in the Department of Theoretical Physics. Going in at the side entrance, he passed Joanna. 'Won't be needing your services now,' he told her. 'The typing, I mean. Did it myself.' Joanna scowled at him. 'Hope you like the stockings,' he said, and skipped up the stairs two at a time. When he checked his pigeonhole, King found a brown envelope similar to the one he was carrying. Someone had sent him a paper. He looked at the sender's name, but didn't recognize it. In his office, he examined the contents.

A Vision of the Universe
by E. Warren B.Sc.

Dear colleague and (I hope) friend,

I send you this in the sad expectation that you, like all the others, will see fit to reject out of hand all my ideas; ideas which are the result of fifteen years of thought. But I earnestly hope that you will at least spare a moment to read my work, to give it a fair hearing, since you are a scientist and a scientist must always approach every new problem objectively. I believe that if you, like me, are prepared to be truly objective then you, like me, will be forced to reject some of the fundamental principles of physics as currently taught, and you will see that the ideon theory provides a new, simpler, unified explanation. As some of the consequences of this theory, let me first list a few:

1. That the speed of light c is not constant, but is a variable $c(x,y,z,t)$, and as a consequence is not the greatest possible velocity;

2. That there are particles (ideons) which can travel faster than light and are the fundamental constituents of all things;

3. That the soul is composed of two types of ideon held in a certain balance, and that death occurs when there is a net flux of life force away from the host;

4. That the infiniteness of the total life force of the Universe proves the existence of God.

In addition, it is easy to derive all of the fundamental constants of nature and the values of the fundamental variables such as $c(x,y,z,t)$. Moreover, given a sufficiently powerful computer, one could calculate precisely how long a given individual will live.

Colleague, I know that my ideas may seem strange, even revolutionary, but do not allow the fear of the new and the love of tradition to colour your assessment. I earnestly hope that you will assist me in finding a journal which will publish this work. The truth can never be suppressed; you may choose to ignore me, the World may choose to ignore me, but I fear that the consequences for the World could be very grave indeed.

Yours sincerely, Edward Warren B.Sc.

King was always coming across nonsense like this; people claiming to disprove Einstein, or use quantum mechanics to calculate the day of the Last Judgement. It seemed that for every professional physicist, there were goodness knows how many oddballs working away feverishly in their spare time – working with all the dedication and enthusiasm of their 'respectable' counterparts – to create their own bizarre alternatives to orthodox science. And King couldn't help admiring such single-mindedness, such confidence in the validity of their efforts in the face of all the evidence. He liked coming across this mad stuff; it provided him with some light relief. But he had never had one sent directly to him; usually he got them second hand from the secretaries when they were addressed to Professor Saunders.

Introduction

This theory is the result of fifteen years of thought, of study, of experimentation, and of persecution. Anyone who has trodden the path of knowledge will know that it is a stony and difficult one, and that there are many pitfalls along the way. Happy the man who can reach the final destination! I should like to begin by mentioning some of those who have helped or hindered me on my solitary journey. First I thank my physics teacher Mr Jack Price, whose chance remark one day long ago concerning the speed of light was the starting point for all that follows. Since then, I have drawn inspiration and infuriation from many sources, among them Einstein, Bohr, Newton, Maxwell, Mach, Schopenhauer, Kant, Plato, Shakespeare and Christ.

No living person has been of any assistance to me whatsoever in my work; among my more vicious and narrow-minded opponents I include Prof. F. Barlow, Prof. T.S. Goodfellow (was ever a surname less appropriate?!), Dr. M. Smith and Dr. P.C. Osborne. The vindication and general acceptance of the ideon theory will be ample compensation for the attacks of these people and others.

This work is dedicated to the memory of my mother.

King's phone was ringing. He heard Joanna on the line:
'Call for you Dr. King . . .'
Then another voice:
'Hello, Charles?'
'Jenny. What's up?'
'Nothing. Just thought I'd say good morning. I didn't have your extension so I got to you through two switchboards. Bit of a palaver.'
'Oh. So you got back alright last night?'
'Yes, no problems. Can't talk much now, Charles – I'm

at work. And I suppose you're busy. I just wanted to say thanks. It was a nice weekend.'

'Yes, I enjoyed it. And thanks for all your work, it's great.'

'The paper? Oh good. It was nothing, really. Let me know when you've got another that needs typing.'

'Will do.'

'Charles, are you alright?'

'Of course. Not the best place to talk, that's all.'

Jenny said she understood, and she'd better go. And she gave King her work number, in case he ever needed it. Then she rang off.

King heard the click of Jenny's receiver, and then the second click as Joanna hung up. And then he put down his own phone and glanced again at the 'Vision of the Universe'.

Chapter 1
The speed of light is not constant!

Einstein's theory of relativity is regarded as a cornerstone of modern physics. Certainly, Einstein was a very great thinker, and he was right to see the fundamental importance of light. But what he was never able to realize is that in fact the speed of light c is not constant.

The scientific proof of this is so blindingly simple that it seems to me a little strange that Einstein should never have noticed it. But perhaps he was too absorbed in theory to pay attention to the evidence of nature. Think of a lens. The light passing through it is bent – and why? Because it has been slowed down! And so the speed of light cannot be constant! So from now on, we must disregard all this nonsense about relativity, and start from scratch.

What an idiot. King brought out his own paper and began the laborious task of writing in all the mathematical symbols and equations which it hadn't been possible to type. When he was finished he checked it through, then took it downstairs to the photocopy room, handing the eighteen pages over to the girl at the counter who gave him the request form to fill out in duplicate. Then she took everything from him and told him to come back in the afternoon.

Charles felt bad about the way he had spoken to Jenny. He had been surprised to hear her voice; it was an intrusion into a place where she didn't belong. And he had responded by being cold and abrupt, when she had come all the way from London to do him the favour of typing his paper. And Joanna had heard everything, so that in addition to feeling guilty he felt foolish as well.

Back in his office, King tried to do some work. For a while he played with an idea which had been in his mind during the weekend; he pushed the symbols around on paper, looking for the spark that would make them start to do something and take over for themselves. But every few minutes he would stop and gaze out of the window, or play with the cap of his pen, or stop to clean the dirt from his fingernails. He had another look at the 'Vision'.

Chapter 4
The life force

We have already considered the quantum values of mass, charge and spin for the fundamental ideons. We now introduce a new quantum number L, which corresponds to the life force.

Any observable can take one of two life-values (alive or dead), and so we suppose these to be analogous to the eigenstates of a spin $\frac{1}{2}$ particle; i.e. we assume that the life force corresponds to a kind of angular momentum in life-space.

King was forming a mental image of Warren. He must have done a degree in physics, and he'd probably also been reading some popular books on the subject; enough to be able to pick up the language, mix it up in his head with some kind of quasi-religion, and then regurgitate it like this. So much effort! The 'Vision of the Universe' ran to no less than forty-six pages. Had he typed it all himself? And this was a top copy. Did he perhaps prepare a new version for every physicist whose name he came across?

And then they would all take a moment's look, as King had, and wonder how far they would have to read to find the flaw that would allow them to dismiss it. The first page! Then forty-five more of futile typing, dreaming all the while that he was another Einstein. He must spend all day scribbling and typing, this Warren. What sort of work might he do? Probably something where he didn't have to talk to many people; sitting at a desk, hatching wonderful ideas that would fill him with such excitement. Then back to some flat where he lived alone with his typewriter and his library of popular physics books, and his endless rewrites of the 'Vision'. A pity to break in on his dreams. Why go to the trouble of explaining that his life's work, this bundle of fantasies which he had spent so much time assembling, was fit only for the waste paper basket?

How strange, though, that every piece of pseudo-physics is essentially the same; the same preoccupations, the same defiant tone, the same rambling style. Just as all physics papers have a required dryness and detachment, this alternative literature has a corresponding passion and urgency – these 'papers' churned out by solitary men who have no contact with the rest of their pseudo-scientific community. Perhaps they should have a journal all to themselves, and conferences, and even a research institute somewhere safe where they could compare notes, and decide amongst themselves what it was that might make one wrong theory better than another.

In the afternoon, King went back to the photocopy room. He showed his identity card to the girl at the counter, and she checked his name on the card index beside her. He watched her as she stooped over it, her varnished fingernails flicking through the cards.

'King. Here we are. Four copies. I'll go and see if it's ready.' Then he watched the rhythmic oscillations of her mincing walk as she went to the storeroom behind. She was out of his sight for some time, hunting for his papers. When she brought them back – the copies and his original – he signed the duplicate receipts and wished her a pleasant day.

Three copies would go to the journal, the original would go for preprinting, and the other copy was a spare. They weren't good – black shadows at the edges of the pages – but they would have to do. He stopped off at the secretaries' office, where Joanna was typing something. He laid the paper on her desk.

'Preprint?' she asked.

'Please.'

'Fine. Leave it there.'

Then in the corridor, he bumped into Henry. 'Afternoon Charles. Going to the seminar? Might be your sort of thing – something about chirality.'

A stilted conversation with Henry, then back to his office – he had left the door unlocked in his haste. He put his copy of the paper, and the carbon, in the top drawer, and tried to do some more work. But there was only half an hour until the seminar, and it seemed so little time in which to get anything done that he soon found himself picking up the 'Vision' again.

and so we see that the ideon field is not unitary, and hence has complex eigenvalues. The imaginary part is responsible for the proof of reincarnation! And this will also be consistent with what was proved earlier; that the time field consists of an infinity of overlapping loops.

The phone rang again. Now it was Robert's voice.

'Charles? Has anyone been to see you yet?'

'No, haven't heard anything about it.'

'I got a call from the police station; they want me to go there.'

66

'For the vetting?'

'I don't know. We'd better not talk now. They said they want my "assistance". I don't think we'd better discuss things over the phone. Sure no-one's been asking you anything? Been in your office? No? I'd better go, Charles. Talk to you later.'

After Robert had hung up, Charles waited but heard no other sound on the line. He stood up, walked to the window, and looked out onto the lawn below. The police wanted Robert's 'assistance'. It had an ominous sound. He turned and went to the door – locked it, and then began to go through every drawer in his office, and every shelf, for any sign that someone might have been there. But how could he tell if things now were any different from before?

He thought about his chair; had it been in an unusual position that morning, relative to the desk? And the waste-paper basket – but the cleaners move that anyway, and the chair. And if someone had gone through his drawers, what might they have found? The only thing with any personal information was his address book, and that was harmless. He took it out and read through it, page by page. If Robert hadn't mentioned Flood he wouldn't even have thought about it; he could have faced any interview with a completely clear conscience, simply because he had forgotten all about it. But because of Robert's paranoia and his bloody book, he was now infected with suspicion. Why had he locked the door?

There was a knock, and he gave a start. When he opened it, he saw Henry. 'Seminar time, Charles.'

8

Charles King and Robert Waters first met five years earlier, in a cafe in Cambridge. It was winter, and the cafe was only a little less cold than the street outside. King was having breakfast, though it was already after ten. He had been with a woman the previous night. When he had first gone to bed with her two months previously, it had been a night of little sleep, and then coffee at seven a.m. in a workmen's stand-up place. Now he would sleep heavily beside her until half past nine.

Sitting at a table, he saw Robert walk in – a young man of similar age to King, slightly nervous in his movements. He seemed to be searching for someone; scanning the dirty tables, then looking at the counter, and asking the girl what they had today. And King saw him glance over his shoulder, in his direction. For a moment, their eyes met, and King felt the stranger searching his face, and he wondered if this man ought to be familiar. He tried to remember where he might have seen him.

King was twenty-seven, and still young enough to be idealistic about the waves of political reform which had begun to fill so many people with hope. Three weeks earlier, he and everyone else had watched on television the speech which now seemed to suggest the genuine possibility of change. Why had one speech been able to have such an effect?

King imagined a situation which occurred during the war. An SS officer was assassinated by the Resistance, so the local commander rounded up a hundred civilians and held them hostage, guarded over by a single machine gunner. They stood huddled in the market square, with only the lone soldier holding them back from freedom. If one person tried to take action, he would be shot immediately. If fifty ran for the gunner, then perhaps a couple of dozen would die before he was overpowered, and the survivors would run free. But the hundred hostages stood and did nothing. If there had been a million of them, watched over by the gunner, would the crowd have wasted a moment over the puny guard? Surely, they would have pushed forward to overwhelm him without a second thought. But what if there had been a thousand? Or five hundred? What is it that can give a group of people the courage to put aside their individual thoughts of self-preservation, so that others might live? Yet each of those hundred civilians stood firm. Each clung to the hope that surviving another five minutes improved their chance of eventually going free. Some time later, the young machine gunner received the command to put an end to them all.

And what, King wondered, if that soldier had made the following humane offer to his hundred hostages: he would spare the first one who tried to escape, but would kill any who tried to follow. What then would be the response? A moment of nervousness, perhaps, and then a stampede.

A nation is oppressed, and does nothing. If one person cries out and protests, he is imprisoned. But then that rare thing appears: a leader who has both power and humanity. And he decides to be lenient with some of those who cry out. Then the stampede becomes inevitable. This was what was in King's mind as he idly watched the anxious stranger at the counter.

He had his back to King, and had decided against food, which King considered a wise choice. This was not King's usual cafe, and he would not use it again. Now the man was paying the girl, and turning round, trying not to spill the cup of tea he held. He looked again in King's direction, and then he came over, paused, and asked King if he knew him from somewhere:

'Excuse me; have we by any chance met before?'

And there was something in the way that this was said; in the slightly nervous tone of the young man's voice, that made King realize that no, they did not know each other, and they had never met or seen each other before. It was only a line.

It was a line which King himself had used with countless women. In cafes like this, or in the street; the neutral testing of a situation. Sometimes they see through you at once and tell you you're mistaken. And there are those who deal with the question as if it were a problem in algebra; searching their minds for the possibility of some forgotten encounter – mentally cataloguing the places where a chance meeting may have occurred, then finally concluding that there must be some mistake. But there are always a few who take it in the intended spirit; no they say, with a perplexed smile, I don't think so – and you throw in a few suggestions and still she says no; she doesn't go to that pub, no she doesn't play tennis, but she does go swimming, and she often visits such and such a cafe, and perhaps you've seen her in the library.

'You're not an historian, are you?'

'No,' said King, 'physics. Why don't you join me?'

Robert introduced himself; he was a lecturer in the history department, and they considered a few possibilities where they might have met or seen each other. Robert's nervous manner made King feel correspondingly more relaxed.

'So you're a physicist? Such a pity there's so little communication between the arts and sciences; I'm sure each has a great deal to offer the other.'

'Don't you regard history as a science?'

'Only up to a point. History is driven by certain principles, and it's our business to see how those principles have been put into effect.'

King's companion seemed rather puzzled that he should be so eager to discard the game of identifying some fictitious previous encounter. King was more interested in pursuing the line of thought which had been evolving while he had watched the stranger pay for his tea.

'And what,' said King, 'are the principles which drive history?'

Robert fidgeted. 'Human nature. Are you sure you've never been to the Red Lion? You really are awfully familiar.'

70

Robert kept looking now and again beyond King's face, into other regions of the shabby cafe; still as if searching for something.

'Are you expecting company?' King asked him.

'Me? No; I sometimes see friends here – sort of place where you're always bumping into someone you know. You don't usually come here though, I take it?'

Charles told him he preferred the one on Union Street, which was more convenient for him – half way between his office and his flat. Then Robert asked him whereabouts his place was, and what was it like (historians were never put very high on the housing list), and did he live there with his family?

'Single, I see,' said Robert. 'Like me – best way to be, I think.'

King didn't want to be thrown off his chosen theme. 'So you're a scientist of human nature, then?'

Robert laughed. 'You can't turn history into physics; it's not a science in that sense. But you've got to be objective and analytical about things – that's the scientific side of it. So refreshing to get a different point of view – you know, we need people like you to keep us on our toes.'

King wasn't listening. 'Suppose a hundred people are held hostage by a lone gunner. Each individual wants to live, but the only way that can be possible is if the crowd charges at the gunner *en masse*. The crowd can only survive at the expense of a few individuals; the simple sum of individual desires leads them all to wait motionless, in the interests of their own preservation, until they're all killed.'

Robert looked still more perplexed. 'In your crowd of hostages, though, there might be one brave man who decides to take his chances and run for the gunner; then the others might follow.'

'I see,' said King, and took a sip of tea. 'But must there always be leaders? If you watch a flock of starlings they all fly one way or the other in unison – but I don't think there's one special bird that the others follow. Sometimes

71

crowds act spontaneously; things happen without any one individual necessarily willing it to happen.'

'But if history were about nothing more than crowd behaviour then you'd stand even less chance of being scientific about it. How can you explain the way a crowd of people behaves?'

'That's my point,' said King. 'And what is a nation, except a very big crowd of people?'

'You scientists are so abstract! History is about facts, and interpreting facts.'

Robert steered the conversation back into the realm of the concrete. They found themselves talking about films, and whether it was better to go to the cinema alone or with a friend. And while Robert spoke, King found the memory rising involuntarily within him of the flesh which had lain next to his the previous night, and the slimy wetness as he had pushed his fingers inside her. Like drawing the entrails of a chicken, once when he was a boy. You could tell the future like that.

When they had both finished their tea, Robert offered to buy more, which Charles accepted. He watched Robert go back to the counter and try to attract the attention of the morose girl.

Must there always be facts? A flock of birds veers to the left, in a great wave – what facts lead to this? A hundred people stand cowed in a market square, or rush in a mad frenzy. A nation does nothing, or rises up in revolt, and then veers to the left or the right. Is there some sequence of events which can explain all this? And if explanation is possible, does this mean the ability to predict what will happen subsequently, or only the ordering of those events into some satisfactory pattern?

Robert was placing a tray on the table. Then lifting the pot; saying he'd be mother. He was pouring tea into their two cups. Plain facts. But what was his aim? Only to prolong their conversation – perhaps. Or else simple thirst, and politeness. But King still had the feeling he had when Robert first came over to him; that Robert had been trying out a line. That Robert had entered this conversation with the attitude with which King would begin talking to a pretty girl in the street. King was flattered by the thought that Robert might find him attractive. And there was something in the way Robert watched him while he spoke which tended to confirm such a motive. The eager way he agreed at certain moments.

Robert was apologising for the tea. 'Horrible stuff in here. Don't know why I keep coming back.'

'Why do you?'

'Oh. Habit I suppose. It's warm and wet. The tea.'

King saw a young man of about twenty enter the cafe. He looked cold; rubbed his hands together, and steam was coming from his mouth like the breath of a horse. He closed the door behind him and walked to the counter. He bought a cup of coffee and went to sit down out of King's view, but now Robert was watching him. King followed the movement of Robert's eyes as the young man walked past and found a table somewhere at the back. And the eyes swung round to meet King's again.

'You're not a musician are you?' said Robert. 'CPO?' Robert played violin with that amateur orchestra; but no, he hadn't seen King there – piano was King's instrument. Robert said they were giving a concert soon, if King was interested. The main work would be the Pastoral Symphony.

'Not one of his best, I've always thought,' said King. 'Beethoven Six, I mean. So repetitive; like sitting on a train and watching the fields go by one after the other – all exactly the same. All those sequences in the first movement; a real bore. It's very overrated – almost as much as the Ninth.'

Robert was outraged. 'The Ninth overrated? How can you say such a thing?'

'The first three movements I love, but all that Nuremberg Rally stuff in the finale – no thanks.'

'Are you saying Beethoven was a Nazi?'

'Of course not. But I think the finale of the Ninth is the very worst sort of populism. Get a nice simple tune and play it again and again – loudly. *Freu-de, schö-ner Göt-ter-fun-ken . . .*'

King swung his arms in march rhythm while he sang, and Robert laughed, but then was embarrassed they might be making a scene.

'Well I think the Ode to Joy is beautiful,' he said. 'It's about freedom, equality.'

'That's just romantic nonsense. It's a third-rate poem set to a third-rate tune. And if it's really about freedom, then why do we keep hearing it on the radio?'

Robert flinched.

'Don't get me wrong, Robert, I love Beethoven more than anyone – all I'm saying is that he made mistakes. But that's what makes him human.'

King could tell that although Robert disagreed, he was taking some delight in hearing these opinions. He was watching King in the way that a child watches a circus artist; waiting to see what comes next – which only made King all the more eager to perform.

'And the Missa Solemnis – a waste of, what was it, four or five years' work. Good in places, that's all.'

Robert was suitably shocked. 'What about the late quartets? What do you think of them?'

King pronounced his judgement: 'Beethoven's finest works, without doubt.' Robert smiled and sighed with relief at the favourable decision.

In music, they had found the common ground that was to form the basis of a friendship that would last until Robert's death five years later.

'Do you ever do any accompanying?'

'Never tried it,' said King. 'Wouldn't mind a go, though. How do you fancy reading through some scores some time?'

Robert agreed enthusiastically, and they arranged that he would bring his violin to King's flat next Wednesday evening. Then King rose and said he'd better be going now, and wished him goodbye. Robert waited behind, finishing the remnants of tea in the pot as King walked

74

out. King fancied he saw him leave his seat and walk towards the young man at the back. And he imagined Robert asking him if, by any chance, they had met somewhere.

A hundred people stand in the market square of a small town. King tried to remember which town it was. Somewhere in Kent, wasn't it? The mayor was later hanged for collaborating.

9

The following Wednesday evening, Robert appeared at Charles's door with his violin and an armful of scores. King invited him inside, and Robert expressed his admiration of the flat's spaciousness, so that King had to explain how he had won the place, in order that Robert didn't suspect some act of bribery towards the Housing Department.

Robert then went straight to the piano and played an A. He put down the violin case which still burdened one arm, and sat himself on the stool. Then launched into a Mozart sonata; rather mechanically, and too quick. He got caught out on an arpeggio, tried the passage again a couple of times, then stopped.

'It's a nice instrument,' he said.

Charles told him it had belonged to his grandmother. 'She was a very fine pianist – I think she could have made a career out of it, if she'd wanted.'

Robert was opening the violin case. The instrument lay inside, swaddled in some soft cloth which Robert was lifting clear of the dark wood, then he picked up the violin and bow and began drawing a few notes. Charles gave him another A from the piano, and Robert twisted the tuning pegs until he became satisfied. Then he played a quick passage of Bach while he warmed up. This sounded very different from the effort he had made on Charles's piano.

Robert put the violin back down in its case, then began to turn over the pile of scores he had brought.

'What do you want to try, Charles? How about Mozart?'

They went through one of the sonatas. It was a new experience for King, holding the strict rhythm and keeping pace with the violin. He was grateful for the simpler passages in bare octaves.

On Saturday, he had seen Anne again; the woman with whom he had lain soundly sleeping before his first encounter with Robert the previous week. He would have preferred to be alone; she showed up at his flat without warning, and then wanted to stay the night. King knew that their relationship was dead. It was like a withered limb which has atrophied to the extent that the only hope is to have it lopped off.

Charles could see the *da capo* approaching. 'Shall we do the repeat?' he asked.

'Alright.' Then the turning back of the page, and again the rising of the theme in plain octaves.

Anne was twenty-four – three years younger than Charles. She was a schoolteacher, and he had met her one afternoon in the Fitzwilliam Museum, where he had gone to think about a particularly stubborn calculation. She was with a party of children; he had watched her as she led them round the exhibits, and she had also noticed him. At first when their eyes met her face was expressionless, or perhaps puzzled. When they passed later she smiled, and was near enough to speak, but only shrugged to express the difficulty of leading a group of excitable children round a boring museum, because someone thinks it's good for them. Then she had armed them all with clipboards and paper to draw on, and they were sent to find something worth sketching. She was standing in a corner while the children were dispersing, and King took his chance to begin a conversation. Two months later, he lay sleeping in her bed until half past nine in the morning.

When King made a mistake he had to pass over it in order to hold the beat – difficult looking passages he would simplify so as to keep time with Robert's violin. Then towards the end of the movement, he proposed playing the second half repeat, to give him another chance; and now things went more smoothly. When the movement came to its final close he felt satisfied. They went straight into the minuet.

King would leave Anne, the memory of whose flesh still

refused to be refashioned into the memory of that first night, or the first moment when he had watched the movement of her body as she walked in the museum, and the bending of her body as she stooped to talk to the children, because King knew that all he felt was a great emptiness, and her flesh for him was only another region of that emptiness – that vast and unending void. He felt the chords repeat under his fingers, and each chord although it was repeated unchanged was nevertheless different, and each chord was a new mystery, and a new thing suggested, and the idea of a new world – of a new life which might be better, somehow. If only life could hold as much meaning as a piece of music! But he would never be able to recapture that mystery, when he had watched her body as she walked through the museum and each movement suggested something unseen, something to be discovered.

And when the theme of the minuet returned it came back renewed. The violin was sounding close behind his ear, swaying behind him as Robert joined with him in the melody. He could hear the rise and fall of Robert's breathing; the sighs barely suppressed. Now he knew Robert as well as he knew this music. And then it was ended, and they were silent.

King needed to speak. 'Not bad.' He turned to look at Robert – in whose face he saw a look of pleasure, and a lifting of the concentration which they had both maintained. Robert agreed; not bad.

King suggested a break before they do anything else – he went to the kitchen to make tea, and again Robert rattled a few bars of Mozart on the piano. Then he felt Robert enter the kitchen behind him; coming close to stand at his side. Robert took the teapot and carried it to the other room. King followed, and they sat down in the two armchairs. King raised the subject of politics.

'Did you see it in the papers today? Looks as if they're going to put a Forum representative on one of the government committees. Only a gesture, mind you.'

'Sometimes gestures can count for a lot,' Robert replied.

'Never underestimate the power of symbols. Even if who-
ever they took had no political influence, he would still be
there – and that's the important thing.'

When they had finished their tea, they played through
two more sonatas, until they both agreed they were feeling
tired. At the end of the last one, as Charles lifted his hands
from the keyboard, he felt Robert's hand on his shoulder.

'Let's stop now,' said Robert. The hand remained on
King's shoulder longer than was necessary to say this.

Indeed, as Robert himself had said; one should never
underestimate the power of gestures. Standing in the Fitzwilliam Museum, Charles had watched a pretty schoolteacher lead a group of children. He had caught her eye
several times. And on one such occasion she lifted her hair
away from her face as she returned his gaze. The next
time, she smiled, and King waited for the moment when
he could begin a conversation. What he now needed was a
gesture that would say to her: Enough.

Robert's hand had rested lightly on his shoulder, and
now it was gone. Robert was once again putting away the
violin with the care which a mother might bestow on her
child, and King was leafing through the pile of scores.
Amongst them was a folder, which he opened, and found
several sheets of handwritten notes.

'Oh,' said Robert, 'don't look at those!' and King obeyed.

'Is it poetry?' King asked. He had noticed the even
spacing of the lines.

Robert blushed, and confessed to having penned the odd
bit of verse, though at the moment he was also doing some
translations of foreign poets, and this was what the folder
mostly contained. He had been working on them in his
office before coming to King's flat.

King tried to ask him about his writing, but Robert was
embarrassed to discuss it, and so turned the conversation
back to Charles.

'Why don't you take up the pen? Your little story about
the crowd of hostages the other day might make an
interesting essay!'

In fact, Charles had already considered this. On Saturday, before Anne had arrived at his door to disturb him, he had begun working on an article to which he had given the title 'The River of History'. There was at that time a brief craze for pamphlets of all kinds. Though still illegal, they were tolerated; and you would find them everywhere – pasted on walls, or lying on a seat when you got on a bus. Left between the pages of library books – even hidden amongst the tins on a supermarket shelf. Anonymous, irrepressible voices, which came from unknown underground presses, or illicitly used photocopiers. Not only on political topics – there would be song lyrics about all the usual things, or gossip – even recipes. It was more than a fad – it was an experiment with limited freedom of expression, and people were delirious with excitement at the idea. Now King wanted to join in – he wanted to make a pamphlet of his essay. He told Robert about it.

'A spring rises in a mountain somewhere; it flows downhill into a valley, where it meets other streams. They merge and form a great river which flows into the sea. If you look at the shape of the river on a map, what do you see? At the coast, there's the thick line which represents the river at its fullest. Go back inland along its course, and you see the river split into its tributaries, and they again split; until you have the feathery pattern of mountain streams which is how the whole thing began. Now ask yourself, what was each stream trying to do? Was it trying to find a river to flow into? No – it was simply responding to the force of gravity, by finding the shortest path down the mountain. Each of the streams does this, and so they find themselves merging in the valley below and producing a river which could provide electricity for a whole town – or sweep away an entire community. The course of the river – from that feathery pattern in the mountains right down to the place where it meets the sea – is dictated by the shape of the landscape, and the force of gravity.

'Now imagine a nation of individuals. Each one is driven by some natural force – the will to survive, to rear children, and so on. Each acts in response to this; yet the result is some great surge in one direction or the other, like the course of the river.

'Or imagine those hundred people and the lone machine-gunner. They all run, or they all stand. In either case, each person is responding to the same instinctive urge, but the slightest difference in circumstances can mean the difference between escape and survival, or else death.'

'But Charles, if you're trying to say that the course of history is like the course of a river, then there's something else you ought to take into account. The river doesn't simply follow the landscape – it changes it. What about erosion, and sedimentation, and all those other things that geographers go on about?'

'Yes, yes of course. But my picture is more complicated even than that. Not only does this "river of history" change the landscape which it flows through, but the landscape itself is constantly changing anyway, because of other factors. You could think of each person as having his own personal "landscape" determined by the way everyone else behaves; and he in turn affects other people's behaviour. It's a dynamical thing.'

'I'm getting lost, Charles. But it seems to me, that you think history can be turned into some kind of equation. I suppose you think then we could predict everything that's going to happen in the future?'

While King was writing, Anne had come to disturb him. And he had imagined two streams, running briefly together, then splitting and following their separate paths down different sides of the hill.

He knew that Robert had not understood what he was saying, but this only made him more eager to finish writing it down, and make his ideas clearer.

'I've got it, Charles. What you're saying, is that we're at a watershed. Is that it?'

'Yes, but what I want to know is how the geography of the landscape is determined in the first place. Why have we reached the watershed now, and not ten years ago?'

'That's what historians are here for, Charles. But I look forward to reading your essay.'

'Why don't you help me? I'm thinking of putting together a pamphlet – we could include some of your poetry. Might be able to find some more people who could contribute on a regular basis. I'm going to call it Flood. How does that sound?'

King had said nothing to Anne about Flood. He and Robert had played a couple of sonatas together, and now he felt he knew Robert better than he knew the woman with whom he had slept a dozen times. He found this thought distasteful, but he could not deny it.

Robert said he'd think about the pamphlet, but that he'd better be going, and would ring soon to arrange another musical session. He took a page from his folder, turned it to its blank side, and casually tore a strip from the bottom on which to make a note of King's number. And he wrote beside it the letters FLO in neat script, like an index in a file. Yes, he said, he'd think about it. Then he stood up, and King showed him to the door. They shook hands warmly before parting.

It was a time of hope; there was a sense in those days that history was about to happen. Like a flock of birds that was swirling, while some unseen force was trying to decide whether to send them veering one way or the other. Yet five years later, all that would remain would be the memory of some tanks, and some brave people facing teenage soldiers. Five years later, Robert would be married to that woman in whose bed King had lain asleep until half past nine. And he would receive a phone call, asking him to report to the police station.

10

'Take a seat Mr. Waters. My name's Inspector Mays; Constable Perkins here is going to take the notes. We think you might be able to help us with an investigation we're carrying out at the moment. Give us the benefit of some of your education. First in Classics and Ancient History, it says here.'

'That's right.'

'Can you read Greek?'

'If that's what you need then I think you've got the wrong man, Inspector.'

'Perhaps. We'll see. But you're obviously a very talented fellow – I can tell why they're so keen on getting you to write this book. What does Anne think about it?'

'My wife? Nothing in particular. I mean, she's pleased. Well, we haven't really discussed it.'

'She should be proud of you. It's a great honour.'

'Yes, but I mean, I'm not really at liberty to discuss it with her.'

'No, I suppose not. You're as well to be cautious. Says here she's a teacher. Should know all about discipline. Are you a believer in discipline?'

'I believe in teaching children right from wrong.'

'And how do you do that?'

'By setting the right example.'

'So what do you do when a child does something wrong?'

'I tell him off.'

'Is that all? There is a danger with that, isn't there? Spare the rod? If you let them get away with little things then they end up doing far worse. You know, some people say that the law in this country is a bit too severe in some cases. What do you think?'

'I think it's . . . appropriate.'

'Always?'

'Yes.'

'Our philosophy sounds a bit different from yours, though. You see, we don't believe in sparing the rod. It's all very well setting a good example, but for some people that still isn't enough.'

'Bringing up a child isn't the same as policing a nation of adults.'

'Really? I'm not so sure. Sometimes adults need to be taught right from wrong. Sometimes they need a rap on the knuckles if they've been a bit naughty.'

'What are you getting at?'

'Does the name Ganymede mean anything to you?'

'Ganymede? No.'

'I thought you had a First in Classics?'

'Yes. I mean it's mythology, not history.'

'History, mythology, it's all the same to me. Don't you know the story?'

'Let me think. Wasn't he the one who was abducted by Zeus, disguised as an eagle? Zeus was in love with him.'

'In love with him. You know what he'd get for that nowadays, don't you? Five years, easily. Not counting the abducting bit. Investigating judge wouldn't be too happy with that either. What do you think about that, Mr. Waters? Five years. Would that be a bit harsh?'

'It's the law.'

'Yes, but do you think it would be "appropriate"?'

'I suppose that society has to be protected.'

'Indeed. Fancy a cup of tea, Mr. Waters? Perkins, go and do the honours. You see, we've reopened an old case. Funny how it happens – something turns up, something insignificant – but it's a bit odd, and it makes you curious. Then you take a look in the files and you find you're onto something. We're looking for someone who used the name Ganymede. Sort of a codename. Any ideas?'

'No.'

'Sure about that? A friend, maybe?'

'I'm quite sure. What's this person supposed to have done?'

'Why don't you tell me a bit more of the story, now it seems to be coming back to you?'

'I don't think there is any more.'

'Zeus kept him as his cup bearer – his catamite, in fact. Don't need a First in Classics to be able to go and look that up in a book. But I also read something about him being put among the stars. I couldn't find a constellation called Ganymede.'

'It's Aquarius.'

'Ah, I see. My wife's birth sign, that. Funny. You believe in all that stuff Mr. Waters?'

'No. But I'm a Libra if you're interested.'

'Yes. We know. Put it there Perkins, that's it. How do they get Aquarius from Ganymede?'

'Water bearer. It's Latin.'

'Of course. Water. That makes sense. Want some milk and sugar in your tea? I'm off the sugar at the moment – the wife has put me on another diet. All a matter of self-control, I suppose. Self-discipline. Are you a believer in self-discipline?'

'I like to think so.'

'Not the sort who'd go discussing classified information with his friends and family?'

'Certainly not.'

'The sort of person who can keep a secret?'

'Yes.'

'And do you have many secrets?'

'No. I mean, this book they want me to work on . . .'

'I'm not asking you about the book, Mr. Waters. You're not here to be vetted – that's for Section Five to deal with. We just need some help in our enquiry. So let's get back to Ganymede. Not a nice story, is it? All about child rape, as far as I can see.'

'I don't know if I'd put it quite like that.'

'Then how would you put it?'

'It's a myth; you're not meant to take it literally. It's symbolic.'

'What does it symbolize?'

'I don't know. It could be many things. There are lots of stories about Zeus carrying people away for one reason or another; often the abduction really represents something more abstract, like being seized by some emotion or idea. And there are other interpretations, of course. The eagle is a symbol of power . . .'

'Of state authority, for example? Seizing a little boy and carrying him away? Taking him into care, say, if his parents were a bad social example?'

'Are you trying to accuse me of something?'

'It's only hypothetical; don't take it personally. You see, I'm just trying to get some insight into this "Ganymede". What sort of person he might be, how he might think.'

'I still don't really understand how I'm supposed to be of help to you. I haven't told you anything you don't already know.'

'But we've hardly started yet. I've still got a lot more questions, Mr. Waters. Maybe not today, though. No rush. You're something of a writer, aren't you? This book, and so on. Do you ever do any other writing? Stories, poems, anything like that?'

'I'm not the creative type. I stick to facts.'

'Then you're a man after my own heart. Finding out the facts, that's what we're both interested in. I think that maybe we have a lot in common. Got any friends who write?'

'Not that I know of. It isn't a crime, is it?'

'Depends what sort of thing you write about. And an artistic personality can sometimes indicate a lack of good judgement in other areas. In the moral sphere, for example. You see, when people are morally weak, it can lead to more serious things. If someone can't be part of normal society, then he feels isolated, outcast. Perhaps all he needs is a little help and guidance. A little self-discipline. Other-wise he might become anti-social, or even subversive. I think "Ganymede" may be in need of some guidance. And I think that you – with your expert knowledge – might be in a position to help us find him.

'But time is pressing, Mr. Waters; you've been a great help to us today. Perhaps when you go away and you've got more time to reflect on what I've said then something more will come to mind that you feel is worth discussing. We can talk about it next time. But for the moment, I'd better let you get back to work – Perkins will show you out. Goodbye for now, Mr. Waters. And give my regards to the family.'

11

While Robert was at the police station, Charles was sitting through a seminar. He found it frustrating and tedious. He felt irritated that he had allowed Robert's anxiety to take hold of him. What was there for Charles to be afraid of?

During the rest of the afternoon, he expected to get another call from Robert, but there was nothing. He checked the three copies of his paper, and wrote out a summary for the Office of Publications. Then he took everything to Joanna, so she could type the summary and send the paper to the Journal of British Physics. He found Joanna alone, fiddling with her typewriter; she seemed to be having trouble with a key that was sticking.

'Do you need a hand with that?' he said.

'I'll have to send a note to Maintenance.'

'If we can sort it out now it'll save you the trouble. Let's have a look.' He bent over the keyboard and began to poke at the keys and levers. 'If you wiggle it about a bit they sometimes sort themselves out.' He was leaning closely over the stubborn typewriter, and so now was Joanna. He could smell the harsh edge of her perfume, and he was aware of her breasts beneath her stiff white blouse.

'Don't waste your time with it, Dr. King.' She didn't move.

'If I can just reach this bit in here – see, it's got a bit bent. See it there?' Joanna leaned in closer to look, and King could almost feel her breath against his cheek. 'Difficult to give it the right sort of pressure from this angle.'

'I might be able to reach. My fingers are smaller.'

'Try not to break a nail. That's it. Just push.'

His dislike for Joanna didn't prevent him from enjoying this moment. As she pushed at the troublesome component, he watched the stiffening of her body. Despite her slightly resentful attitude towards his interference, she was nevertheless happy and willing to go through this little piece of flirtatious theatre.

'There, you see?' He tapped the key several times and watched the lever rising again and again to stamp its letter on the empty roller.

'Thanks. You've got quite a way with these machines, haven't you?'

'Pity I can't actually use them.'

'What about your paper? You said you typed it yourself.'

'Oh, yes. What I meant was, I got a friend to do it.'

'And did you have to bribe her as well?'

'Look, Joanna, I didn't mean any offence with those stockings.'

'None taken. I was simply too busy, otherwise I'd have done it. And they're nice stockings. Let's say I owe you one.'

'Alright. Let's. And in the meantime, maybe you could type this summary for Publications, and send these off.'

'I think I can manage that. Leave it all there.'

'Right. Oh, and Joanna – do call me Charles.'

Then he went upstairs to the tea room, where a few people had gathered after the seminar. He avoided the speaker, who was in deep conversation anyway, and took a newspaper from the rack. Then he sat down near Henry, who was scribbling equations on a napkin and explaining something to one of the postgraduates.

Charles found himself thinking again about Jenny. It wasn't a good idea if she came to see him in Cambridge too often. He didn't like it when the various compartments of his life began to overlap and interfere with each other.

Economic prospects remain good. Charles glanced at the photographs in the newspaper of new factories, and new government appointees. The purpose of the newspaper was to reassure its readers that nothing was happening; that while individual events could be interesting or even sensational, they could never threaten to bring change. The purpose of the newspaper was to pretend to be a newspaper; to present trivia or downright falsehoods in the form of stories.

Steady road to prosperity. Charles's purpose in taking the newspaper from the rack was so as to pretend to read it; so as to be immune from conversation while he drank his tea, and thought about Jenny, and thought about Robert's absurd anxiety. Black newsprint was already smudging his fingers.

Film Review: Harvest of Angels (Cert U). Clive Rentford stars as wartime Resistance hero Bob 'Winner' Winmore in this vivid account of the farmer's son turned freedom fighter. William Dangerfield puts in a superbly menacing performance as Steuermann, and look out for Peter Ray as Moseley. Romance is provided by the ever lovely Annette Hughes as Winmore's sweetheart Dora. Recommended.

With Jenny, King had only ever wanted sex – nothing else. And the usual pattern in an affair like this was that after a while, he would inevitably begin to get to know the woman; find out what she was like as a person. And this would dull his interest – he would find that there was nothing there which would make them be friends. Because the women whom King wanted to sleep with never seemed to be the sort of women with whom he might want to maintain a friendship. But he was beginning to find that he liked Jenny. She seemed honest, and vulnerable. And also willing to give him whatever he wanted. This frightened him. And then she had turned up on his doorstep on Friday night, with wet hair, because she had come all the way from London to type his paper. His relationship with Jenny gave him a feeling of power, and this was what was so frightening. She would never deny him anything – it was up to him to draw the line.

*Radio choice: In Conversation (*Home Service, Fri. 9 p.m.*). The new Minister for Justice, Reginald Thornville, discusses his long career, including his role in the drafting of the Constitution in 1947. More recently he has been Chairman of the Committee for Public Rights. Among his choice of records are Mozart's Clarinet Concerto, Schubert's Trout Quintet and Beethoven's Ninth Symphony.*

King turned the pages as if he were paying close attention

to the newspaper. He finished his tea, and went back downstairs to his office, sat at his desk and stared at the pile of blank paper which lay in front of him.

Jenny frequently asked him about his work. She said she couldn't imagine what it must be like to do nothing but calculations all day – as if she saw him as some kind of computing machine, or perhaps a glorified accountant. When he tried to describe to her his typical day, he realized that only a comparatively small part of it involved putting pen to paper. Mostly he would be reading, or thinking, or gazing out of the window. Which sounded to Jenny like time wasting, though that wasn't the way he liked to see it.

And then she asked him how he could be a physicist if he never did any experiments, and he reminded her that Einstein worked that way too. But still she couldn't imagine how King could derive any pleasure from all these incomprehensible symbols and formulae he spent his time mulling over. So he told her it was all a bit like doing a jigsaw, or a crossword puzzle, where you spend so much time feeling horribly frustrated and longing desperately for the stroke of inspiration that will give you the right place for a piece, or the right word for a clue. And then you make another step forward, and for a moment you feel like a genius, until you find yourself stuck again. And so Jenny asked King if he saw the world as a great puzzle, and he said that he did, although part of the puzzle was to try and find out exactly what sort of puzzle it was.

After three quarters of an hour of calculation, King had turned a one line equation into a sum of terms which covered a page and a half. Then he started collecting coefficients, and cancelling things out, and after a while he found himself left with zero. So he stopped in disgust, walked up and down for a couple of minutes, and then had another look at the 'Vision of the Universe'.

using expression (57), we see that souls are inherently fermionic, and so by the Pauli exclusion principle we cannot have two souls simultaneously occupying a single body. Thus, the practices of certain 'churches' concerning possession and the exorcism of spirits are seen to have no possible scientific basis.

Finally in this chapter, we give another proof of the existence of God. The full Lagrangian for the ideon theory is given by equation (63). This leads in fact to divergences, and for renormalisation we add a new field which couples to everything and cancels these problems. This universal field is God.

There was a knock on his door. It was Joanna; she wanted Charles to explain something he'd written in his summary.

'What's this word here?' She had placed the manuscript on his desk and was leaning over him, pointing at the offending scribble. King closed the 'Vision' and pushed it to one side.

'Asymptotic,' he said.

'You'd better spell it.'

He wrote it again for her. 'That alright?'

'Fine. Don't know why you physicists always have to use such long words for everything.'

'So that people don't know what we're talking about.'

'I can believe that. Oh by the way, Charles, I sent your paper downstairs for preprinting. Should be ready by Wednesday.'

'Thanks.' He watched her close the door behind her. Charles, indeed! She'd almost tripped over the name as she said it, obviously so eager to be able to use it.

Now Joanna would send the three copies of the paper, with the summary, to the Journal of British Physics. Then the Journal would send one copy with the summary to the Office of Publications – a formality, although this was the government department which had the final authority on everything which was to go into print. And the Journal would send another copy to a referee, who would decide whether it was worth publishing. Such was the procedure which every paper had to go through before it could be accepted.

King was at home that evening when he got a phone call from Robert.

'How did it go at the police station? Not too much of a grilling, I hope.'

'Oh, no. I can't really talk now Charles. I was wondering if you're doing anything at the weekend; I was thinking of taking Anne out for a drive – I can get Madge to look after Duncan if his cold doesn't clear up. You could bring Jenny.'

'Splendid idea. Are you alright Robert? You don't sound too well.'

'No, I'm o.k. Charles. Bad line. I'll come and pick you up on Saturday morning. How does eleven o'clock sound?'

'That's fine. I'll call Jenny tomorrow and see if she can come up on Friday evening.'

'Yes. And Charles . . . Don't say anything to her. You know what I mean. Better go. Bye now.'

Charles knew from Robert's voice that things hadn't gone well. He dialled Robert's number, but it was Anne who answered. No, Robert wasn't there – he went out for a walk, about half an hour ago. And when King dialled Robert's office he got no reply. Robert must have gone out to a call box for fear of tapped lines. And he had been so brief on the phone, not wanting to discuss anything. All of this alarmed King; he felt nervous and restless that night. He wanted to speak to Robert to clear it all up, but he decided that Robert must know best, and he should wait for him to call or visit. He slept little.

Next morning, Tuesday, there was another large brown envelope in King's pigeonhole.

A Vision of the Universe: Supplement

Dear Dr. King,

I await with interest your comments on my paper, 'A Vision of the Universe', which you will by now have had time to read. I enclose some further results concerning the ideon theory, including an important

Conjecture which, if true, greatly simplifies the proof of Theorem 6. However, I cannot yet verify this Conjecture (although it is so plausible as to be blindingly obvious). As soon as I can, I will of course inform you of the argument. In the meantime, please consider it proved.

Dr. King, as a respected scientist I greatly value your judgement, and your assistance would be of inestimable value. Though you may be burdened already by work, I would implore you that the importance of the ideon theory for the World is such that any delay in spreading it to the widest possible audience could have very detrimental and unfortunate consequences for Mankind. Thwarted as I have been already by such cosmic bastards as Smith and Goodfellow, I now turn to you in a last desperate act of hope. Please do not betray the spirit of science in the same manner as those venomous charlatans.

Yours sincerely, Edward Warren B.Sc.

King put this fresh sheaf of nonsense on top of the previous day's offering, then picked up the telephone and called Jenny's work number. A frosty voice replied that Miss Lindsay was busy at the moment, and when he said that this was Dr. King speaking, and could Miss Lindsay please call him back, the frosty voice thawed a little – no doubt wondering what ailment Jenny might have, or if she might even be pregnant – and said that Doctor could be sure that the message would be passed on straight away.

Then King returned to the calculation which had defeated him yesterday. He had another idea, which had come to him while he was walking to work, and using this he soon had another page and a half of terms to simplify.

The phone rang, and he heard Joanna put Jenny through to him.

'Charles? They said you rang.'

When he spoke to her before, he had felt inhibited by the thought that Joanna was probably listening to the conversation. But now he took a strange kind of delight in the idea. He asked Jenny if she could come up to Cambridge again on Friday, and she said she'd love to. She could stop work early, and arrive as soon as he liked. Then King thought about it; he said he didn't know if he might want to work a bit later on Friday . . . He'd leave a key for her, so she could let herself in whenever she arrived – it would be under the mat at the front door. Then on Saturday they'd go out with Robert and his wife.

'You mean the awkward one?'

'You'll like him when you get to know him. He's a very good friend of mine.'

'In that case I suppose he must be alright. See you on Friday, Charles.'

King listened for the click of Joanna's phone after Jenny hung up, but he heard nothing.

For the rest of that week, there was no word from Robert.

12

On Saturday morning, Robert arrived at precisely eleven to collect Charles and Jenny. Jenny saw from the kitchen window the white car pulling up outside, and the three figures emerging; Robert whom she had found so abrupt during their brief meeting the previous weekend, and his wife – a serious looking woman, slightly taller than her husband. And their young child, grabbing at Robert's hand.

When Jenny had arrived last night from London she found that Charles was still out. The key was under the mat as promised, and she had let herself in. It was cold and dark inside. Switching on the lights, she had seen everything again as she had remembered it. When Charles returned, he would find the flat tidied. The small bunch of flowers she had bought at the station would have sprung from the empty milk bottle which she would have rinsed out in the kitchen sink.

Jenny found it hard to believe that they – she and Charles – were really no more than two chemicals meeting in an experiment. Already she felt she knew him well enough to see how complicated he was, and she wondered if this was to do with the fact that he knew so much. Perhaps by thinking all the time about everything, you only end up confusing yourself. From the kitchen window, she watched the white Morris Commonwealth pull up in the bright morning sunshine.

She had had two hours by herself before Charles returned on Friday night. At first, she had the feeling that he would arrive at any minute; she had busied herself in the bathroom, freshening herself up. Then there was time to find somewhere to put the small bunch of flowers – no vases anywhere; on the shelves, it was mostly books. Books in at least three different languages, and even those in English had incomprehensible titles. The only ornaments were those souvenirs from foreign travel – the Russian samovar, the absurd cigarette lighter in the form of the Empire State Building. Jenny was glad that Charles didn't smoke – so much better for the lungs. But there were no vases. She finally settled for an empty milk bottle, which she rinsed out in the kitchen sink.

By then, half an hour had passed without Charles appearing at the door. Jenny wiped the cooker, still stained from the lunch she had made last Sunday. Then tidied the rest of the kitchen, and the sitting room, and eventually the whole flat.

When she had finished, she sat down on Charles's bed. It didn't creak as much as her own; it was softer, seemed deeper. When she sat on it, it quivered beneath her. Lying on this bed, with Charles pushing down on top of her, she had felt herself being buried in mountains of softness.

She opened the wardrobe and looked at his clothes, his shoes. And the chest of drawers; his horrible old socks and underwear in the top drawer. Some ideas for birthday presents. The second drawer: sweaters. And in the bottom – she knew already – old papers and letters.

Now it was Saturday morning. Looking out of the kitchen window, Jenny saw the car, bright in the early sunshine, and then the three figures coming up the path and disappearing from view down below. Then the ringing of the doorbell; Charles let them in. Jenny could hear the voices of Charles and Robert, and the quiet voice of the woman. She dried her hands and went to say hello. Robert seemed a little friendlier, though still rather formal. Jenny stooped down to kiss the little boy – Duncan, only four years old. He turned and hid his face in his mother's leg, which made everyone laugh. And his mother – who only smiled when she made a deliberate effort. Her name was Anne. But nothing about her appearance that might suggest she had been Charles's lover.

In the car, Charles sat in the front next to Robert, while Jenny and Anne had Duncan between them in the back.

The men in front were discussing the best route to the village where they would have lunch. Jenny felt the need to make conversation with the other woman.

Anne had been a teacher, then stopped to have Duncan. She hoped to go back to work eventually. Jenny found her manner cold; she told Jenny only the facts of her life, and none of the feelings.

Robert was looking at Jenny in the rear view mirror. 'And what exactly do you do, Jenny? Charles hasn't told us very much about you. Civil service, isn't it?'

No, she told him, the Electricity Board.

'And how do you like living in London?'

Well enough, she said. She thought about her tiny flat in Bayswater, with its narrow slice of kitchen, and the bedroom defined only by a curtain. They were out of the town now; all around was flat, open countryside.

Robert caught her eye again in the mirror. 'You get away from London much?'

'Whenever I get the chance.'

'Nice to get away to visit friends, eh? Do you know anyone else round here?'

'Other than Charles? No.'

Robert suddenly braked to a halt. There had been a thump at the front of the car. Jenny felt herself being thrown almost into the back of Robert's head.

'Damn,' said Charles, 'I think you hit it.' Robert parked by the verge, and got out. Charles followed. At the side of the road further back a rabbit lay dead, its open mouth deep red with blood. Charles touched its warm body, then kicked it into the ditch. 'Some supper for the foxes,' he said. 'You alright, Robert?'

When they got back into the car, Duncan was still asking what happened. Anne was telling him a bunny rabbit had run in front of them, and now it had run away home into the bushes.

'Why did the rabbit do that, Daddy?'

Robert started the car and set off again. 'I don't know son. Expect he was just crossing the road.'

From her back seat, Anne spoke quietly. 'Perhaps you should go a little slower round here.'

They stopped later on for a walk; Robert knew a good place. It was warm for October – too warm for a coat. Anne helped Duncan out of the car, and asked Robert to fetch her camera from the glove compartment. Jenny went up to Charles and put her arm round him. He moved away, as if to admire the scenery. He began talking to Robert, and soon the two men were walking far in front, out of earshot.

'So how did it go at the police station, Robert?'

'They know about Flood, Charles. There's a man there called Mays, he asked me all about Ganymede. I don't know why he didn't come straight out and accuse me – I think he was trying to catch me out.'

'What did you tell them?'

'Nothing. But they know, Charles.'

'It's possible that they don't regard it as sufficiently serious to take any action.'

'Yes, it's possible. But be very careful, Charles. You can see why I didn't want to talk on the telephone . . . Ah, what have you got there, son?' Duncan had come running up to them with a piece of leafy tree branch he had found. 'Have you shown it to Mummy?'

Duncan said he had, and walked beside his father, clutching the end of Robert's jacket.

Jenny and Anne were walking together some distance behind. Anne was asking her how she and Charles had met. Jenny said it was in London, but didn't want to admit the story of the bicycle and the conversation in the street.

'It was through a friend.'

'Ah. Another physicist?'

'No; you probably wouldn't know her.'

'A female friend, I see.' Anne laughed. 'How many girlfriends has he got in London?'

Jenny said nothing. Sitting on Charles's soft bed the previous night – no sign of him coming back. The temptation to look through his things. Those things in the bottom drawer. *Anne.*

Duncan was running around now looking for more pieces of tree branch.

'Do you think they'll want to interview you again, Robert?'

'I expect so. Look Charles, it's you I'm worried about. If they want to do anything about Flood, then they may be after you.'

Charles was biting at his lip. 'How the hell could they have found out? Do you think they knew about it all the time, and this book of yours has brought it to a head?'

'Oh, that's lovely Duncan. Go and show it to Mummy. Charles, I don't know. There was nothing they could have found when they searched my office; I destroyed everything to do with Flood a long time ago. I think the only explanation is that someone has given them some information.'

'But who?'

'Someone close enough to one or other of us to be able to find something out. Strange, isn't it, that it all coincided with Jenny's arrival here last weekend.'

'Oh Robert, don't be stupid.'

Behind them, Anne was looking at some red flowers which Duncan had pulled up by the roots. 'Do you come to Cambridge every weekend, Jenny?'

'This is only the second time.'

'You haven't known Charles very long?' More than two months, Jenny told her. 'The beginning is always the best time,' said Anne, 'isn't it?' She was twirling the red flowered stems between her fingers. Duncan had lost interest in them now, and was looking for something else.

Sitting on the edge of Charles's bed; reaching down to open the drawer. *Missing your body. Anne.* A card from the Fitzwilliam. No date.

The two men were still far ahead.

'Charles, think hard. Is there anything you might have told Jenny about me, or about Flood?'

'It's not the sort of thing I would discuss with her, Robert. I hardly know her, really.'

100

'Has she ever been alone in your flat?'

'No. She was there last night . . . but you were interviewed on Monday.'

'She was with you all of last weekend, wasn't she?'

'Yes – hardly out of my sight. She spent most of the time typing my paper.'

'Where was she when she was typing?'

'In the sitting room, at the dining table. I played piano for her.'

'All day?'

'No, not all day. We did other things.'

'Like what?'

'Use your imagination, Robert.'

'But not all day, Charles. Was there any period of time when she was in your flat and you didn't know what she was doing?'

'Well, I could hardly be watching her the whole time – but Robert, what could she have found?'

'Have you still got a copy of Flood somewhere?'

'I don't know – oh, Robert, you can't honestly expect me to begin suspecting Jenny; she wouldn't hurt a fly. Do you want me to start spying on her?'

'We don't know that she isn't already spying on us. She happens to get nosy in your flat. She happens to find something – she gets frightened, she realizes there's a side to you she doesn't know; that you once wrote subversive pamphlets. She wonders what she's getting involved with – it frightens her, Charles. Makes her aware how little she knows you. It works on her imagination – the next day she takes it to the police.'

'No, she couldn't have taken it to the police.'

'Did you see her off at the train station?'

'For God's sake Robert, what are you talking about? What evidence . . . ?'

'Charles, they know about Flood. They can do what they like with us now. They had to find out somehow.'

Further behind, Jenny and Anne were talking about Duncan, who was trotting along beside them.

'He starts school next year. I might go back into teaching then.'

'Do you think you'll have any more?'

'I don't think so. I'm happy enough with things as they are.' But Anne didn't strike Jenny as a happy woman.

'You met Robert through Charles, didn't you?'

Anne's face flushed. 'Is that what Charles told you?'

'He only mentioned it – that he was a mutual friend.'

The two men had stopped ahead at a gate. Duncan ran to them, and then the women caught up. The gate was fastened with a padlock and chain. Charles offered to help them over.

'Are we allowed?' said Anne.

'Don't see why not.' Charles had already climbed over it. 'Do you want to take my hand, Anne?' Jenny watched as the other woman reached out for Charles's grip; his free hand reaching for her side as she swung over the top of the gate. Then Robert helped Duncan over, and now it was Jenny's turn. It was alright, she told Charles, she could manage.

'Perhaps we should only go a little further,' said Anne; 'Duncan's looking a bit tired. Then we could go back to the car and drive on for lunch.'

'I'm not tired, Mummy!'

'But I'm sure you'd like some lunch, wouldn't you?'

'I'm not hungry.'

They carried on. Robert and Charles now lagged behind.

'So what do you want me to do, Robert?'

'Be very, very careful. Make sure there's nothing that could be used against you – search your flat from top to bottom, before someone does it for you.'

'Do you really think they'll take any action?'

'It's up to them. There still might not be much hard evidence – even if they had a copy of Flood from your place, there's no proof that either of us was involved. It would only be possession – a fine, perhaps.'

'But it was you they questioned about it; how did they know you were in it too?'

Robert slowed down a little. 'I've got a theory about that. When I went for the interview, they said it wasn't about the vetting; they wanted me to help them find someone else – as if it was a completely separate inquiry. Then they asked me all about Ganymede. I think they might want me to give them information about you. If they had a copy that Jenny found in your place, then they'd want to know where it came from; who wrote it, distributed it and so on. And so they would want someone close to you to find out as much as possible. To inform on you. I think that's what they wanted from me. Though of course they'll get nowhere with me.'

'But then there's Jenny.'

'They can use all sorts of pressure, Charles. There must be God knows how many ways they could blackmail her into helping them. Is she married?'

'Don't be stupid.'

The women had stopped again. Duncan was saying he was tired, and he wanted his lunch now. Anne suggested they turn back.

Duncan sat on Robert's shoulders while they walked back to the car. He had a long piece of grass in his fist, which he used to tickle the heads of the others. Only Jenny seemed interested in this game; she would walk in front of Robert, and from his high position Duncan would play the stem of grass on Jenny's hair, until she would pretend that there was some unknown irritation on her head which she would reach for blindly. The walk back to the car went quickly. Nobody said much.

PART THREE

13

The train journey from Cremona to Milan takes me nearly an hour each way, Monday to Friday. A long time to spend on a train every week, but better than having to live in Milan. And it gives me ample time to do my writing – already we have reached Chapter Thirteen, and I've been at it barely a month! At this rate, it will all be finished before summer.

I have always loved trains; my earliest memories are of my father taking me to watch the steam locomotives puffing along the tracks which must have been near the house we lived in then. Of that house, I have only the barest of recollections; a pattern on the stair carpet, or the scrolling plumes of steam once from an unattended kettle (which made me think the house and our belongings might all be burned to the ground). But the visits to the railway line are much clearer in my mind. We would watch from a hill the line below us, within view of the signal further up the track. All would be quiet, and I would wait, like an angler watching his float, for the twitching of the signal blade. 'Singal! Singal!' I would shout, then soon afterwards an engine would come chugging past. I would wave with the hand that wasn't held by my father, and I would see the driver look up and wave back. I see them still, those drivers – or perhaps it's only a single engineer that my mind has preserved, then repainted with a dozen different faces and gestures – but the one I see most vividly had blue overalls and a cap, and even from the distance at which we stood, I could see the dirt and grease on his face and waving arm. And perhaps this is part of the attraction of trains for little boys – that the job of engine driver is one in which not only are you allowed to be dirty, but it is your duty to get as dirty as you possibly can.

Precisely what my father did during these visits, I do not

know. For me, he was at those moments nothing more than a mute anchor, holding me at the crest of the hill in case I should slip or decide to run in my excitement. The trains, I see now, could have held no interest for him; his only delight could have been my own pleasure. I wonder if he stole those moments by the railway track in order to be alone with his thoughts. Perhaps if I had ever had children of my own, I might have been able to discover an answer.

But Eleonora made it clear from the start that the role of mother was something for which she was no more suited than I was to be a priest. And it's not the sort of thing you can get round by arguing and debating. Sometimes I felt as if I had won her over; I would watch the way she admired the children of others, or spoke about pregnant friends. But the charm of others' children, I realized, was precisely that – that they weren't hers.

I first met Eleonora on a train not unlike the one on which I am now sitting. It was not long after I had first settled here; still my foreignness and bad Italian made the smallest things a great effort requiring a good deal of thought. It was a relief to me to find myself sitting alone on the train, not having to try and make myself understood. But when Eleonora came and sat on the row of seats opposite mine, and politely acknowledged my presence, I felt a greater than usual desire to put my thoughts into words – those, at least, which I wished her to hear.

I talked to her about the state of things in Britain, and my reasons for giving up my life there for exile in Italy. And I explained to her that whereas in my home country I had been a lecturer in mathematical physics, I now earned my living by giving English lessons.

She said she lived in Milan, and could I take her as a student, and I decided that although I was already committed to more teaching than I would like, I could still fit her in – say, on Friday evenings. She found a scrap of paper and wrote down her details for me, and this was when I learned her name: Eleonora Cosini. Like Zeno, I said (I had once attempted Svevo's masterpiece), but she didn't pick up the allusion, and so I made nothing more of it, since my aim was to seem sophisticated rather than clever. And then I said it reminded me of *cosine*, and she agreed it was the sort of name to appeal to a mathematician.

I shan't tire you with a lengthy description of Eleonora. Imagine a woman who seems striking and intelligent rather than conventionally beautiful, and whose manner manages at once to beckon and to forbid, and you will have as good a picture of her as I can paint. I didn't think at the time she was the sort of woman I could love in the warm sense, but her coolness came to fascinate me. And the years we had together before she passed away proved to be a time of happiness – only now that she's gone do I realize quite how happy I was.

But now we're already at the first stop, and some people are getting on. Perhaps my habit of writing only on the train is not such a good one – the constant interruptions mean I'm forever losing the thread. I want to carry on the story of Duncan and Giovanna, but already I'm forgetting what was happening to them, because I always begin each journey with a sheaf of blank paper (otherwise I might lose everything one day, which would be very unfortunate after so much work), so it's difficult for me to go back over what I've already written. Under such conditions, a certain amount of repetition or self-contradiction is inevitable. But this needn't be a cause for too much inconvenience; is life not full of anomalies and contradictions? It was only in mathematics that I was ever able to find any degree of consistency with which to console myself, but I gave that up twenty years ago.

Most other travellers use the time to read – newspapers or books. But I never read newspapers, and with books I have always had an uneasy relationship. I'm attracted by a good title, or an attractive cover. And I'm particularly careful to check the number of pages before I part with any money, because if there's more than three hundred there's little chance of me ever getting to the end.

Although, of course, the end is always the first part I look at; being left-handed, my way of flicking through a book is to begin by opening it at the last page then leafing back to the start.

If I find a page or two which seem interesting, and if the book satisfies all the other requirements, and if I have enough money at the time (I often fall at this final hurdle) then I buy it, and spend an hour or two in the evening totally engrossed in the fictions which the author chooses to parade before me. Taking the book with me on the train next day would be futile – I know I would end up gazing out of the window, or else reading the same page from top to bottom a dozen times or more – none of it making the slightest impression on my imagination – while my mind would slip away of its own accord towards some more interesting topic. And so I leave the book at home, patiently awaiting my return, when I pick it up and try to get back into the state of excited involvement with which I had lain it down.

But getting back into a book is rather like crawling into your unmade bed – what was warm and inviting, and fitted perfectly your needs, now seems cold and stale. You twist and turn, you writhe and fidget; the book now has lost some of its appeal. Still I persevere, but the following night I perhaps decide to take the evening off; the book lies forlornly on the arm of the sofa with the marker hanging limply from somewhere near the front. Eventually, after a few more evenings of desultory page turning, I will put the thing out of its misery, and consign it to its grave on the shelf. In this way, I must have read the beginnings of a thousand novels, and never managed to persevere with more than a dozen of them.

And this life of literary promiscuity – constantly hopping from the pages of one writer to those of another – has its effect on my own attempts to write. Because always when I sit myself on the train with the paper wedged against me in defence against the jolts of the carriage, it's the voice of the writer who last spoke to me which fills my mind, more so than whatever I put on paper during my previous journey – and this, coupled with my natural tendency to seek approval through imitation, inevitably leads me to try and modify my own voice accordingly; each day a new act of ventriloquism, as one book after another is sent to the sagging shelves and forgotten.

Eleonora, on the other hand, was an avid reader; she consumed books with all the passion and enthusiasm that I might bestow on a good steak – and just as I am with food, so was she with her reading; she could never leave a book without digesting every word, to the very end. Sometimes I would find her sitting with her feet up (in those awful slippers) and she would tell me what a dreadful book it was that she was currently immersed in. A day or two later and she would still be there, wading uncomfortably through the pages, until at last she would pass final judgement on it – the opinion which she had already formed before reaching the second chapter.

I think often of Eleonora – I'm surprised by the memories which choose to appear, at the most inappropriate moments; things I had totally forgotten about. But it's difficult to take the train each day without sometimes remembering what it was like when we first met. The thing which prompted our initial conversation was the book I was reading – the *Racconti Impossibili* of Alfredo Galli. In those days, twenty years ago, I still made the pretence of reading on trains since I felt it was somehow good for me. I had already read Galli years before in Britain; it was one of the few books which I actually wanted to finish, and – having finished – begin again.

Eleonora sat down opposite me, and although I had been happy to sit in silence, I now felt a strong desire to express myself as fluently as I could. She smiled politely to acknowledge my presence, and I wished her good day. I could see at once that my foreign accent had made some kind of impression; her eyes flickered like the pointer on a sensitive instrument. But she said nothing more. Her eyes flicked down to register the cover of the book I was reading. Later I was to realize that she had chosen to come and sit in this compartment – which was occupied only by a solitary man, myself – because she had noticed that I was reading Galli, and this aroused her interest. I like to think that what she really meant was that she found me attractive, and felt she would be able to use the book as the pretext for a conversation. In any case, the book was responsible in one way or another for the fact that I met Eleonora, and she became my student, and then later my wife. What, I wonder, might have been the outcome if I had been reading Moravia, for example?

But the infinite chain of accidents by which the world proceeds are not a great cause of wonder for me. There are those who regard the chance events which shape their lives as indicative of some kind of destiny; as if, for example, it had been ordained that Eleonora and I should meet in that particular train on that particular day. More reasonable, though, to take the view that the pinnacle of random happenings on which we sit only means that we ourselves are accidents of fate. The train on which I was travelling when I first met Eleonora was simply what I caught when I missed the previous one by a couple of minutes – and my emigration to Italy was itself more or less an accident. Going further back, was it not mere chance that should have chosen me as the offspring with which my parents should have been blessed? How many other human beings might equally well have been produced by them with equal probability (considering the myriad thousands of seeds which each would attempt, with every coupling, to lead to the creation of a new life)? There must have been enough possible alternatives to my own existence, I don't doubt, to populate a small town. Add to this the fact that my parents didn't even want another child, and it becomes clear to me that it's surprising that I'm here at all. And given that I do exist, it's equally clear that my life could have taken any number of directions, but the countless nudges which have pushed it one way or the other have for the most part been insignificant, and are now impossible to recall.

It was Eleonora who began our first conversation, on that train twenty years ago; during one of my many spells of inattention she asked me what I thought of the book, and was it worth reading, and then wanted to know where I came from. And so I told her my story, and how I was now earning a living by giving English lessons. And so she became my student, and then later my wife. I like to think of her, reading a book with her feet up. And those awful slippers.

What, I wonder, would my father have made of the woman I married? I disappointed him in so many ways. The fact that we produced no offspring would no doubt have provided another instance of this.

How sad it must have been for him, when every father longs only to see his child grow up to do better than himself in every way; yet he could only watch me fail to reach one after another all the high standards which he set for me. Perhaps during those visits we made long ago to the railway track, he thought about all the possible futures I might have; as many and various as all the alternative children my parents might equally well have produced in my place. But Nature chose me, and I chose Eleonora.

It was not my intention, however, to speak of her, or of my father. I wish to return to the story of Duncan and Giovanna. All I remember is that it wasn't going at all in the way that I expected when it was a tale which lived only in my imagination. Strange, that the act of writing should deflect one's ideas so much from their proper course – I thought I knew by now how I wanted to fashion that opening scene, and yet once I actually began putting pen to paper, it soon wandered off in quite the wrong direction. Sadly, I can see only one solution to the problem. I shall have to start again.

14

It sounded no different from pushing an old, empty car down over a hill in order to get rid of it; the speed at which it had approached the bend, and the efforts of the driver to save himself – if he had had time to make any – did nothing to alter the impression that it was only useless junk which was crashing heavily in the darkness through low bushes. And the hillside was being littered with the contents of a suitcase – socks, underwear, trousers – and the contents of a briefcase also, or perhaps a file or folder – papers were being scattered.

And when Duncan wasn't looking out of the window of the train he was reading a story by Alfredo Galli.

For three days, Lorenzo had watched the car on the Via Salvatore, and the inexplicable movements of those whose world it overlapped. Those for whom it was not simply another parked vehicle, but for whom it had purpose, and significance.

For three days, he had watched in the hope that there would be some gesture, some manifestation of meaning in the scenes which his binoculars revealed to him – those spasmodic vignettes, framed by a circle of darkness, as one after another the passers-by entered and then left his field of vision, until at last he would see once more one of those whom he had come to recognize. There were two of them – a man and a woman. There was no logic in the times when they might choose to appear, but he had seen them repeatedly. One or other would come near the car, and hesitate as if waiting for something. Their movements made little sense, and yet he faithfully noted everything he saw; made a detailed record in his small black notebook. That the two were members of the June the Seventh Brigade seemed now to Lorenzo to be quite certain. All that remained, was to wait and see what it was they were going to do.

And when Duncan wasn't reading, he was staring out of the window of the train, and thinking again about his father. Only the barest of memories – Duncan was just four when he died. And yet that half-remembered figure, hazy and god-like, has been watching over him ever since.

His father sitting at his desk, rattling away on the typewriter; or playing with him on his knee. Hard to say how much was really remembered, and how much invented. But whenever these pictures surfaced, Duncan felt once more inside himself that anger which would never leave him until he could find out exactly how, and why, and who.

Duncan's mother took him to live in York after it happened – Cambridge had too many memories for her. And it is there that his own recollection of the past begins to crystallize into something having order and coherence. The many times he asked her to tell him about his father – what he was like, what he wore, did he smoke a pipe? And the gradual discovery of clues.

For three days, the darkened hotel room had been Lorenzo's world – his only interest, the scene he saw through the binoculars, of the street below. Quite what Lorenzo's life consisted of, does not concern us here. Whether he thought of his wife and children, or imagined himself to have a wife and children where none in fact existed – does this make any difference to his silent vigil? If he were to die in the course of duty, would it matter if he were to be mourned by many, or by none? And what difference also would it make, if those who mourned (supposing there to be any) were not informed of the true facts of Lorenzo's death (since it would all have to be kept utterly secret), but were told instead that he had met an unfortunate accident?

His father had just begun writing a book when he died –
an official history of revolution in England. Somehow, this
fact seemed crucial. He had gone to Scotland to work on
it, and crashed shortly after he began the journey back to
Cambridge.

Duncan's mother would never say much about it; over
the years, Duncan had to work on his own theories. And
gradually, a story emerged in fragments. He knew that
Charles King, his father's closest friend, left Cambridge to
live in Leeds soon after the accident, and it seemed that
perhaps he might know something. But Duncan's mother
was reluctant to have any contact with King and his wife,
even though King tried to keep in touch. Which only
made Duncan all the more eager to ask him about it.

Now Duncan saw that the train had reached the first
station, and people were getting on. A foreign girl asked
him if the seat opposite was free, and then sat down.
Though he would have preferred to have been left alone
with his thoughts, and his book.

Lorenzo could check the hour not only by his watch,
but also by the clock on the bank across the street.
And he soon came to know how the changing of the
hours was reflected in the changing light of the street,
and the changing pattern of traffic which moved
through it. Sitting patiently by the window, he began
to feel that he too was part of some great cycle of
which he had previously been only vaguely aware.
He saw the arc of the sun each day as it crossed the
narrow strip of sky above him, and he thought of the
earth's slow rotation, and the gradual turning of the
seasons, and the unending course of birth and death in
the midst of which he found himself, a single lonely
soul, linked mysteriously with the two people who
came and went and revealed themselves to the lenses
of his binoculars.

When Duncan was old enough to go to university he was

given a place at Leeds to study history. King suggested that Duncan come and live with them, and despite everything his mother said to try and dissuade him, Duncan was keen to have such an opportunity of getting to know the man who had been so close to his father.

But he soon found that whatever King knew about the circumstances of Robert Waters' death, he would reveal nothing. It seemed almost as if King had something to hide.

'I see you're reading Alfredo Galli.' The girl is speaking to him — and although Duncan makes no more than a minimal response, she seems disposed to continue. 'I read the *Theft*; that's an interesting book. It's about two people who never meet. She works in a library, and he always comes in on a Friday, which is her day off, and every week he steals a book. You know, Galli has this idea that our whole life is just a story, and there are all these other ways the story could go, but they somehow get stolen from us. It's a nice idea, I think.'

While she speaks, Duncan is reminded of the image (photographed, in lurid colours) of the father who had been stolen from him, and the life which had been stolen from him. Yes, he says, it's a nice idea. And he returns to his book.

15

Two of them – a man and a woman. Young and good looking. Lorenzo imagined them to be lovers; there was no evidence for this, it was a thought which entered his mind and remained there with the spurious weight of fact. Nevertheless, it was not difficult for him to weave around them a myriad of lives which would explain how they had come to be involved in this sordid business. He pitied them both; they looked so ordinary – gentle, even – and yet he knew that they must be implicated in acts of callous violence.

That anger; diffuse and unable to be directed or controlled. The car tumbling – the callous violence of this act. The white Morris Commonwealth crashing through the barrier. And the refusal of those who understood it to admit their involvement.

For three days, Lorenzo observed patiently, making all the while a careful note of what he saw. He never left his hotel room, except to go to the toilet further along the corridor. And he made sure that whenever he did this, there was no-one else about, who might recognize him. While he was in the hotel, it was as if he no longer existed – as though he had been temporarily removed from the world, in order that he could be nothing but an unseen pair of eyes.

Three times a day he would hear the trundling wheels in the corridor, of the trolley on which his food was brought. There would be a knock on the door, and then the sound of the trolley moving away. When all was quiet, he would open the door of his dark, curtained room, and the artificial light of the corridor would meet him. On the floor, he would see his meal on a tray. If his surveillance continued long enough, then no doubt he would begin to detect another level in the hierarchy of recurring cycles. He would begin to identify the days according to the menu.

King's refusal ever to discuss the matter – almost as if he were hiding something. But it was plain that the crash could not have been an accident (no other vehicle involved, no witnesses). And the sheaf of typed notes, dirty and crumpled, which were sent back afterwards (supposedly those found at the scene) – these could not have been the work of Robert Waters.

Had Duncan any wish to talk to the girl sitting opposite him, he might have told her his theory about the crash, a theory against which he still had found no contradictory evidence:

Robert Waters was working on an official book; a privileged position for which he would have needed security clearance. Secret papers would have been open to his inspection. And in the course of his work he found out more than they wanted him to (what might he have found out?). He wrote about things they didn't want discussed – refused to play the game of rewriting history to suit the Party. He became dangerous to them; and so they had to kill him. They sabotaged his car; made it crash, then stole all his notes – all his dangerous discoveries. They picked over the wreckage on the hillside, and cared nothing for the man they had killed (or left for dead). All they wanted were his papers. And the ones which were sent back weeks later – those crumpled pages – were the work of a third-rate hack; a parody of Robert Waters' style. Perhaps it was written after the crash, in an office somewhere, then made to look soiled. Or they might have prepared it all beforehand, then stood on the hillside in the night, beside the overturned car, and thrown the sheets one at a time into the drizzle, for someone else to find. Perhaps this is how it was.

119

But Duncan had no wish to talk to the girl. He told her none of this.

For three days Lorenzo had been living amongst the shadows of his curtained hotel room. He had watched the two suspects come separately to the car – stand near it; pause and look around. The man might light a cigarette; the woman check her watch. Each would hesitate purposefully. Why should they wait like this, beside the car? What event did they expect?

The refusal of everyone to talk about the crash – all too scared for their own skins, in those days. But now at last the old order had fallen, and all the files had been opened. King didn't want Duncan to go. 'We all did things in those days we'd prefer to forget about.' That's what he said – or something like it. So that they got into that stupid argument.

The ticket collector is coming down the carriage. Duncan brings the ticket from his wallet, and the girl reaches for her bag.

'Thank you. Right. There you are love. Thank you sir.' The scrutiny of the ticket collector. 'Ah. You've got a white saver here.'

'Yes. It's a white day today, isn't it?'

'No, it's pink savers or standard fare today sir. I'm afraid you'll have to pay the difference.' The ticket collector consults the yellowed pages of his fare manual. 'That's another two pounds please.'

Duncan looks in his wallet and finds a one pound note and four shillings in change. The ticket collector offers to take his name and address so he can send the money. The girl butts in.

'Please, how much do you need?'

'Oh, no, it's alright.'

'Please, what do you need? I have two pounds, look. Take it, please.'

She insists, so he takes six shillings; the collector pockets the money and moves on. Duncan offers to pay it back, but knows he never will.

'You know,' she says, 'in Italy it wouldn't be enough to buy a stamp.'

This is meant to make him feel better, but instead it only reminds Duncan of how poor he must seem to her.

'I left myself a bit short,' he says. 'I spent more than I intended while I was in London.'

'Ah yes, I noticed there are a lot of foreign goods in the shops now.'

'It wasn't shopping that did it – I had to pay to see some files.'

The Office of Public Records was not the sort of building Duncan had expected. Smaller than he had imagined. And only a shabby waiting room for the public, with a wooden counter at one end, and a glimpse of filing cabinets, rows of them, stretching from floor to ceiling. But only a glimpse. This was nothing more than an antechamber. This was nothing more than the part they allowed you to see, and hence automatically insignificant.

At first no one, then at last a clerk appeared, and took the details from Duncan's identity card before he could even explain why he was there. And then Duncan said it was his father's file he wanted to see, and the clerk told him you could only see your own file, unless you had a court order. And to Duncan, these grinding obstacles seemed all too familiar. Bureaucracy is always the last thing to change.

He waited for a quarter of an hour while the clerk went to look for his file. When the clerk came back, he told him there was nothing in his name, and Duncan felt almost disappointed. Then Duncan said again that it was his father's file he was interested in, Robert Waters, and the clerk told him again that in that case the normal procedure was to obtain a court order first. And when the clerk mentioned the 'normal procedure', Duncan realized that nothing had changed. He asked the clerk if he could at least tell him whether a file on his father existed, and the clerk said that he could go and look, but there would be a fee. How much? The clerk was looking at Duncan and trying to guess his worth. One pound, he said. And would any part of the file be open for inspection without a court order? The clerk rubbed his chin and thought about it. Perhaps; it would depend. And would there be a fee for that as well? Oh yes, said the clerk, of course. And now the clerk scribbled something on a piece of paper, and looked at it earnestly, and thought for a moment. Five pounds, he said, and I'll bring you whatever I can.

The clerk took Duncan's last five pound note, and went away again. Duncan sat down on the bench and waited, staring at the varied yellows and browns of the stained walls. The clerk had probably gone away to read the newspaper while he tried to make his mind up whether he could screw this one for any more. But five pounds is a lot to hand over in one go. He would have to come up with something.

Half an hour later, the clerk came back again behind the counter. Now he was carrying a grey folder, like a slim box. He told Duncan to step through the side door and follow him. They walked in silence along a narrow, featureless corridor, Duncan's shoes squeaking on the floor as he kept pace. Then they reached the reading room, where an attendant sat dozing in a corner. The clerk put the file on the long table in the centre of the room, told Duncan to give it back to the attendant when he was finished, and then left. Duncan sat down and opened the file. A bundle of papers was held down by a clip at the side which he loosened so as to lift out the sheets.

'Sssst!' The attendant shook his finger at him. There was no one else in the silent room, but the attendant acted as if they were in a crowded library; using only angry gestures to make Duncan realize that he must not remove anything from the file.

But Duncan soon realized that things already had been removed; the page numbers were haphazard, and reference was made to items not present. The clerk had probably kept back most of the contents so as to earn himself some more money later on. What was left told Duncan nothing new. There were the bare facts; date of birth, places of residence, employment details. Then part of the report from the inquest: his father was driving alone, and he had left the road at speed, going through the barrier and down the hillside. Death from multiple injuries sustained during the crash. All documents found at the scene had been given security clearance and released to the next of kin. No other vehicle involved, and driving conditions good, although the road required care, particularly at night. Verdict: misadventure. All of this, Duncan knew already.

His journey to London had been a waste of time. He would have to go back again once he could afford a bigger tip for the clerk. He had no desire to tell the foreign girl any of this. He heard her voice:

'Do you know if there is somewhere to get a cup of coffee?'

Duncan said he thought there was a dining car further along, and when she asked if he wanted anything he declined. If six shillings was the price of a postage stamp, she could probably afford to buy dinner for the whole bloody train, but Duncan wanted to be alone. He watched her make her way down the aisle of the carriage.

16

Lorenzo had been waiting already for many hours before the woman made her appearance once more from around the corner. Then he followed with his binoculars her moving figure (the swing of her walk, no different from any other pretty girl) until she came past the car, and hesitated exactly as expected. She was looking in her handbag again; rummaging inside it. A set of keys brought out – and she was opening the car door! Lorenzo felt his heart thumping inside his chest. After three days of patient observation, something was happening at last. The binoculars trembled in his hands as he watched her unlock the car door and get into the driver's seat. Now she was sitting behind the wheel, and adjusting the rear-view mirror. A young woman – soft and gentle features. Adjusting the mirror – through the binoculars he watched her movements. And then as if for no reason she turned her face upwards. What impulse might have prompted this? She turned her face upwards, and Lorenzo found himself staring, through the lenses of his binoculars, directly into her eyes.

That car – half-remembered smell of leather seats. Things swinging inside; the motion of the car. White car, your father driving; the back of your father's head. Thin slice of memory. Your father's voice.

She was looking at him. Across that great distance, Lorenzo felt sure that the face which stared in his direction could see him – could see a pair of binoculars poking out from behind a curtain. He felt petrified. Her face – her pretty young face – was turned upwards towards him, and he imagined that he saw now on her lips the curl of a smile. Only the briefest of moments, and yet during it he felt frozen, and exposed. He felt her eyes discovering him, unmasking him, and undoing all his work. Only the briefest of moments, but at last he pulled himself away from the curtain.

The room was dark, despite the bright sunshine outside, and he felt the darkness spinning around him. He felt the danger of his work, and the folly of believing that he could carry it out without the world ever noticing him. When he was once more calm enough, he dared to look again. The car, and the woman who was driving it, had gone.

Approaching the bend. Night. How would they have done it? The brakes perhaps. Car braking suddenly — what was that? Only a rabbit crossing the road. Warm bodies beside you in the back seat of the car. Looking down at your shorts; your own pink legs swinging. Grown-up legs on each side of you. Precious wedge of memory.

For the rest of that day, Lorenzo saw nothing. In his notebook, he recorded the events he had witnessed, but also he gave vent to his feelings of rage and frustration at his failure. He recorded all his theories and suspicions, as if his ingenuity might somehow compensate for such crass stupidity when he had allowed his quarry to escape. During most of the night, he remained awake beside the window, looking down upon a street in which nothing happened.

A sickly dawn broke at last. He got up, and went to the toilet. Standing inside the narrow room, the bright light made his tired head ring, and the sound of his own water thundered in his ears. He felt wretched and nauseous.

When he returned to his room, Lorenzo looked out once more into the street. Nothing had changed; the car still had not returned. He went to take his notebook and record the fact. And this was when he found that his notebook was gone.

125

The white Morris Commonwealth hitting the barrier, and all his things coming out of the door when it flew open, when it was pulled back on itself and crumpled under the body of the car then reappeared as the car turned again, the door flapping like an injury and the suitcase, the briefcase. The typewritten papers. Your father driving – back of his head. That memory. And trying to make him turn; to see his face, make him speak and live again.

Many thoughts would stream through his mind during the hour which followed – scenes in which he would imagine how the woman, or one of her companions, had entered the room and taken the book. Scenes of the way in which they might now choose to deal with him – a lonely figure, anonymous and unmissed; a figure taken out during the night, unheard by the staff who did not even know his face. Images in his mind, during the hour which followed, of those two people whom he had watched so closely – whom he felt he now knew – taking him, his hands bound behind his back, with a blindfold across his eyes. His terror, a sensation beyond fear – a strange new realm of calm, where he would wait (what sweet images might he try to think of?) until at last the dull thud would meet the back of his neck and he would die without hearing the report of the gun, or smelling the smoke from its barrel in the cold night air, and his lifeless body would feel nothing as they bundled it into the boot of the car.

It would be an hour rich in thought – an hour such as he had never before known. And during that time, he would go once more to the window, and throw back the curtains behind which he had hidden. He would look down onto the deserted street below – the street whose every corner he knew so well – and he would see only the twisted lines of his own handwriting; the meaningless lines which had betrayed him. And in his mind he would recreate again and again that place where they might take him; the woman going into the building first, and then the other leading him blindfold – he would be led stumbling in terrified darkness up unknown stairs. Apologizing perhaps for his own clumsiness. Into the echoes of a bare room, where his feet would shuffle on the floor-boards beneath him and he would hear the cocking of a handgun.

How many of them were there? Difficult to tell – two or three might have been enough. Perhaps one of them would have remembered to check that he had not survived, or would not survive. The back of his head, washed with rain and blood. His head, turned and lifted by a gloved hand. Then they would take out the sheaf of typed notes they had been given and throw them, a handful at a time, into the air so that in the darkness the breeze would catch them and they would fall naturally amongst the trail of clothing, metal parts and other rubbish.

It would be an hour such as he had never known. And at last, at the end of it, what urgent thoughts might fill his head as he gently turns the catch on the window of his hotel room? And what words must remain unspoken – words of explanation and apology – as now he lifts himself out into the cool air; eases himself out over the blind, uncaring street far below and balances for a moment, unseen, on the high window ledge? And what fear, or calm joy beyond fear, holds him there now between life and easy death – the only escape from the unimaginable torture of his pursuers?

He will fall in that early morning with the swiftness of ripe fruit. And in the street which he has watched and come to know so well, and of which he now becomes a lifeless part, there will be none to see him.

17

The cyclical view of history is a mysterious one, and many have been perplexed by it. That the disasters and tragedies of the world should be doomed to undergo endless repetition – is this not a terrible prospect? Again the rise of ruthless dictatorships; again the massacre of innocent people; again the bloodiest of wars. It is a depressing thought, yet who can wholeheartedly deny it? Was the Great War not described at the time as the War to end all Wars? There was no shortage of hope in those days. All that was lacking was a little imagination.

It is easy to see why the doctrine of reincarnation is such a deeply rooted one. If misery must return again and again, then must it always be experienced by new souls? Can souls not be recycled in the same way as history? And perhaps when our souls return the next time they might fare better.

The cyclical view explains a good deal about our own lives. A man and a woman meet, they have an affair, and at the beginning they don't stop to think that what they are experiencing is the same as all the other affairs they have had. Then later on things go wrong, they part, and each feels that things always happen this way. They are reassured by a cycle of their own making.

We then have an image of the world as a certain limited repertoire of patterns with which to make sense of events. We could say that if history seems to repeat itself, it's only because historians – using the finite vocabulary of history – must eventually repeat themselves. How many words do we have for 'war'? How many ways do we have for explaining the breakdown in relations between two people, or two nations?

We could take this a little further. Lowell tells us that the brain is made of a huge (but finite) number of cells, and a thought – a 'state of mind' – consists of a particular pattern of electrical impulses between these cells. The number of possible patterns is more than sufficient to give us a lifetime's worth of thoughts and experiences. But if we could live forever, would we not one day run out of new thoughts? Would we not eventually exhaust the finite number of states which our brain is capable of achieving? And then we would surely be doomed to the perpetual re-experiencing of former mental states. If immortality exists, it is an endless, recurring agony of nostalgia.

How often I have had the thought 'We have been here before.' It seems to come more and more frequently with advancing years. Perhaps my brain is simply running out of new ways to comprehend the world. Even so, the temptation becomes increasingly irresistible, to view the world as a tangle of overlapping cycles. Do we not look at those younger than ourselves and see in them the replaying of the themes which we have spent our own lives inventing? And if nations could grow wiser as well as older, would they not regard their younger fellows with a degree of wistfulness?

When I first arrived in Italy, I was particularly eager to visit the ruins of Pompeii. Since my earliest childhood, I remembered seeing pictures of the place; it had been a great ambition of mine to visit it for myself – and I was not disappointed. What I recall most vividly was the sense that here was a single moment in history – a single day in the year 79 A.D., which had been captured, forever. A moment which posterity could relive again and again. Just as I had seen photographs of these ruins, now when I saw the ruins themselves I was looking at another kind of photograph. And looking at this image of the past, one could see the sense of pride that this town had felt, a part of the greatest empire there had ever been. Now, that empire was itself nothing but dust and rubble. And the plaster figures in glass cases – the casts of those who had been buried under the ash – here were more instances of time frozen. These had been people, like me, and their world had vanished, just as mine would. Was my own soul nothing more than a part of that great unending cycle which had once given them life?

I had heard that some of the figures were kept from public view, so I asked the attendant if I might see the others, and when I gave him a tip he showed me another case, kept in a storeroom, containing the effigies of a couple making love, who had died while locked together in that final embrace. How poignant, this moment of intimacy preserved forever! Beneath the ash which killed them, their bodies had decomposed so that all that was left was the space where they had been. Then, two thousand years later, plaster was injected, and their shadow was cut out by labourers. Perhaps the labourers had laughed when they saw what they had found. Or perhaps there were only one or two of them present, and they might have allowed themselves to feel, as I did, the sense of terrible mystery which the scene deserved.

But the civilization which inhabits the Italian peninsula, for all its antiquity, can lay no claim to greater wisdom over other nations. The cycles of history are a wiping clean, a purging of the past; like the amnesiac woman who saw her husband every day as if it were for the first time. Again, a convenient – and necessary – component of the reincarnation myth is the assumption that all traces of the soul's former life should be erased. Which makes one wonder just what it is that identifies a soul, since our only personal identity in the absence of our bodies is our memory.

I remember standing amongst those ruins, in heat of an intensity I had never before known. I had been living in Cremona for three months, earning a living by teaching English, and my weekend in Naples and Pompeii was the first holiday I had been able to afford. I remember it occurring to me as I stood amongst those ruins that the city of Pompeii had suffered the fate of a film star who dies tragically young – caught forever in its ancient youth; eternally fixed in that moment of blossoming. Of course, the inhabitants knew they were living in the shadow of a volcano; they knew that one day it would explode and destroy everything in its path. But they stayed - they were all able to live in the belief that whenever it happened, they would not be around, and in the meantime they were happy to make the most of the good soil. And now some of them are immortalized in glass cases; the rest are gone and forgotten.

That couple in their eternal embrace, those pathetic white figures, remained in my mind as I took the train back to Milan. I was thinking of them still, though trying to read, when Eleonora (as I was to learn her name to be) came and sat opposite me, and we began a conversation, in which she asked me to give her lessons in English.

Is memory a sort of burial in ash? I see our two bodies, mine and Eleonora's; hers white and smooth, mine – how do I see my own? Indistinctly; since the image cannot come from the memory I carry within my head, but rather from a memory which hovered somewhere above us – I am looking down on the two of us. Perhaps what I see is my present body, my own ageing shell lying next to the smooth white flesh which she still occupied in those days. Not so much a memory, as a photo-montage of how it must have looked, on that Friday evening. Only the second lesson!

Is memory perhaps the injection of substance into a void? I see our two bodies, motionless. Looking as if they would be cold to the touch. Two people begin an affair, and for a while it is like the discovery of a new continent. And then familiarity creeps in; the recognition that things are always this way.

And yet we were married – and the secret of success in our relationship was that we were never in love. Therefore, we could never fall out of it. Not that I didn't *love* Eleonora – I did, dearly; and I miss her painfully. I loved her as I might love a certain piece of music; something without which my life would be poorer. And is poorer. I was never *in* love with her, that's all. Why should I feel any guilt at the omission of one simple, unmissed ingredient?

I see our two bodies, on the double bed which seemed to fill the bedroom of her apartment. I had achieved, at that stage, only one of my goals.

Watching the movement of her face, her hands, her body as she spoke to me on the train, I tried to imagine what it might be like to be in bed with her. Alongside my struggle for correct Italian vocabulary, there were visions of twisted sheets, fingernails clawing, neatly piled hair falling loose. The woman sitting opposite me had such poise, that I wanted only to see her lose her balance, and collapse beneath me.

And I saw that twin effigy in white plaster, writhing yet immobile; that baroque contortion of limbs long dead. Eternal emblem of futility.

Who lives now in that apartment, I wonder, where I gave Eleonora two lessons in English before we pulled each other onto the rug which some friend had brought from Turkey? Who now lies in that bedroom which I came to know so well? I see them now, their young and hopeful bodies, in an endless, anonymous embrace.

Easy to see why the doctrine of reincarnation has always been so attractive. But if one day my soul should once more meet Eleonora's, how might I recognize her?

The cyclical view of history is a perplexing one, but comforting. That all our mistakes, although they will be endlessly repeated by others in the future, have also been made countless times before us by our predecessors – this amounts almost to a pardon. Not an explanation, but an excuse for not finding an explanation.

When I was younger, I feared that my life might become no more than the repetition of my father's; that I was something moulded in his image – the same creased brow, the same receding hairline patiently catching up with his shiny scalp. Inherited mannerisms which sometimes might serve to remind that I was his offspring. When I reached his age, I would be like him. Such certainty depressed me terribly. Yet now that I am drawing nearer to the age at which his own life ended, I regret that I could not have been more like him. The idea that a life could consist of the repetition of another is no longer a depressing thought for me.

I remember how he used to criticize my piano playing; I would read through a new piece and strike plenty of wrong notes. The second time, I would make the same errors – and eventually, as I learned the piece, I would learn those wrong passages as if they were part of the music. If you repeat the same mistake often enough, perhaps it becomes no longer a mistake.

But even if you play a piece a thousand times, no two performances can be exactly alike. My life has been a playing out of themes on which my father had already exercised his virtuosity – how similar in many ways, and yet how different. And if at the end of life there is some kind of *da capo*, I am sure I shall return to make all the same mistakes once more, in new ways.

And although I have tried my best to begin again the story of Duncan and Giovanna, the situation only seems to be getting worse – I am even further from the story which lived in my mind for ten years, after its abrupt arrival one night while I stood naked in my bathroom. I long to bring those two people together, and yet with each attempt I make, they only grow further apart. Again and again, wrong notes come and send the melody adrift. Even now, it seems, I still feel the presence of that guilt which hung over me through the years while I secretly wrote and rewrote the opening scene in my mind. That sense of betrayal, and the questions which Eleonora would have asked me: Who was this Giovanna? So that I would have had to tell her about that other, unknown woman I once met; and all those speculations of how my life might otherwise have gone. When I return to their story, will I be able to make things go any better? Already this novel, like my life, has set off on a path over which I have only the vaguest pretence of control. But tomorrow I shall follow once more the story of Charles King and Robert Waters, to find out where it might lead us.

PART FOUR

18

Twenty years ago, when Charles King was in his early thirties, he would leave his desk in the Department of Theoretical Physics and go home every lunchtime to spend an hour playing the piano. It was a time which was very precious to him, this hour alone at the keyboard. It was the one time during the day when he could escape from the need to think. Sitting himself down with a score in front of him, he would launch his hands into motion.

It was Monday – two days after that walk in the country, when Robert had made him begin to feel suspicious of Jenny. He had said nothing to her about it; she had taken the train back to Cambridge the previous evening – again, she had offered to stay until this morning; again, he had said it was best for her to go and get a good night's sleep before work. And as soon as she had left, he went to his bedroom, and opened the bottom of the chest of drawers, and began rummaging through those papers and old letters. Hard to tell if anyone had looked in here – how would he know the difference? But then he found what he was looking for; deep beneath piles of torn envelopes – two copies of Flood. He drew them out; found himself immersed in his own former words.

A river begins from countless tiny streams. Eventually, it becomes an unstoppable flood. Obstacles put in its path can only avert its course; they cannot stop the great natural force which drives it to its goal.

The force for change – for freedom and justice; these are unstoppable forces of nature. A great dam is built; for decades the flow is held back, but day by day the reservoir of discontent grows steadily deeper. And now the water is beginning to seep over the battlements. What will happen next? Will the dam withstand the constant trickle of fluid over its poorly built walls, or will it give way, and collapse?

Walking back to the car, no-one said much. They drove on for lunch, and the village where they stopped was one of those places which seems to have gone unchanged for centuries – though of course, this was all a fiction. The place had been completely rebuilt after the war. That night, King found himself unable to let Jenny out of his sight for a moment. She knew something was wrong, but couldn't get him to talk about it.

At the piano, his hands move mechanically as his eyes follow the notes.

If change is nothing more than a law of nature, what then is the responsibility of the individual? Should we all wait calmly for the inevitable to happen? Surely not. But the desire for freedom lies within us all – even those who oppress us. We are all slaves of the landscape of tyranny which we have created for ourselves. How was it that this landscape came into being? What is its geology?

They had lunch in a make-believe village reconstructed after the war. A monument on the village green commemorated fallen heroes. To be a hero means to die on the right side, at the right moment.

They sat at one of the tables outside the pub; Duncan drinking orange juice through a straw. Charles wondered if the tension he detected between Jenny and the others was only a manifestation of his own suspicion. Perhaps it was really he who was tense.

In the landscape of tyranny, we can imagine mountains of oppression, summits of persecution. Each individual longs only to flow down to the peace and tranquillity of the valley, and the force which pulls him is the will to survive. To scale one of those peaks of injustice – to speak out and resist, and suffer the consequences – there are few who are brave enough to do this.

But Charles felt sure that Jenny had no hint of the conversation which he had had with Robert. She was fussing now over little Duncan, while Anne looked on in silence.

At the piano, King's hands move mechanically as his eyes follow the marks of the score. Last night, he could hardly wait for Jenny to leave, so that he could search through his papers. And then he had found himself immersed in his own former words.

A thousand tiny streams trickle down mountain sides, and year by year the solid rock is slowly carved away. What once seemed mighty soon begins to look fragile and insubstantial. What once seemed immutable, is seen to be transitory and ephemeral. Power exists only where fear exists, and the river of human will, which is gathering force day by day around us – this flood of hope, will surely sweep away all the fear which may try to block its path.

In the drawer, there were two copies of Flood – two of the photocopies he had made in secret, like a naughty schoolboy. He had never thought to regard it all as much more than a prank. Difficult to tell whether anyone had been through this drawer – so long since he himself had opened it. The pamphlets had been right at the bottom, beneath a pile of other things. Hardly likely that Jenny would have been able to take them out, show them to the police, and bury them in here again without King noticing. Though there could have been a third copy.

Each one nothing more than a few sheets stapled together – a couple of articles, and the poems which Robert signed 'Ganymede'. King tore both copies in half, then quarters. Now it was difficult to tear through the wad; he took the individual pieces and ripped them further. Went to the bathroom and flushed it all down the toilet. As he did this, he had a sudden vision of the drains being cleared in search . . . Absurd idea! But when the flushing water ceased its tumbling, most of the shreds of paper were still floating in the toilet bowl. He waited until the cistern fell silent, tried again. But again this failed to carry them away. So now he reached into the water and pulled the pieces of paper out, a handful at a time. Later, when they were dry, he would burn them in an ash-tray.

Hands moving mechanically over the keyboard. A theme and variations. He hardly hears them.

They had all sat outside the pub in a make-believe village. It was in a village like this that a hundred civilians stood in terror under the guard of a young machine gunner. And then he received the order to end them all.

Duncan spilled his glass of orange juice; sticky liquid spread across the table. Anne mopped it up with a handkerchief. Afterwards, they went back to the car for the drive home. Anne produced her camera, but it was Jenny who offered to take the photograph; the three adults, and little Duncan, standing in front of the white Morris Commonwealth. Those serious expressions. Jenny laughed as she aimed the camera – Charles and Robert forced a smile while between them Anne scowled.

When the torn scraps of paper were sufficiently dry, Charles put them in an ash-tray, a few at a time, and lit them with a match. Soon there was nothing left but cinders and smoke. He had to open a window. He felt now, that he had done all he could – he would have to wait and see what happened next. It was absurd to think that Jenny could betray him – he couldn't see what reason she might have for doing such a thing. To improve her chances of getting a better flat, perhaps. But she didn't seem the type – no more curious than women usually are. Charles looked again through the piles of notes and letters in the bottom drawer; lifting out slabs of paper and envelopes in an attempt to find some answer. Though what he wanted to discover was precisely the thing which he could not possibly hope to find – the proof of her innocence.

Those old letters – letters from friends and colleagues, letters from relatives. Neat letters, or ones scribbled in haste; letters which had lost their meaning, which had lain unread perhaps for years. Letters which formed tangled interlocking mats, like geological strata. The gradual un-earthing of the past – and the search for some answer, some meaning. Letters from lost friends. Letters gone cold. A card which Anne once sent. *Missing your body.* All of this, he would also destroy. Why save any of it?

Their serious faces. Jenny stood with the sun behind her; they all squinted in the sunlight, as she took the picture. Duncan wanted to know if they would see that rabbit again, while they were driving home.

The movement of his fingers. How many times has he played this music? He hardly listens to it.

The drive back to Charles's place to drop him off with Jenny. Robert reluctant to come in for coffee, but in the end they're persuaded, for a while. After they go, Charles and Jenny left alone with the tension between them. Jenny asks him if he once had an affair with Anne. Feminine intuition, she calls it. Then Charles felt relieved by the thought that her suspicious behaviour was only because of her fears about Anne. His relief seemed to wipe out all the doubts which Robert had managed to raise in his mind. He told her not to be silly; Anne wasn't his type. When they went to bed, their sex was like an act of apology. For the rest of that day, and then during Sunday, nothing more was said about the matter.

Old papers, and all those letters – who would have thought there could be so many? All those old messages – and the forming of a pattern, like an archaeological excava-tion; time retreating with increasing depth.

Their sex was like a ritual of atonement. How could he have let Robert stir up such worries? Moving on top of her, a sudden memory of Anne. Trying not to think; to act like a machine without thought or will.

Hardly a wrong note today. Only when he thinks about his hands do they sometimes begin to falter on the keys of the piano.

A machine without thought or will; impelled, after

Jenny left next day, to go and search that bottom drawer. To satisfy himself. A whole night and day spent waiting to open it, to sift through it. He had never let her out of his sight. As a precaution.

The drawer heavy and stiff, as if it had not been pulled open in a long time. The papers at the top pushing up and preventing the drawer from sliding. Packing them down with one hand, to remove the obstacle. Far enough now to reach everything inside. Hands buried in torn papers. And from somewhere near the bottom, two copies of Flood. Then King found himself immersed in his former words.

That river which will sweep away the endless tyranny of lies, and the acceptance of lies, and the power which can exist only because of the weakness of others.

And after everything was burned he went back to the drawer – searching more carefully now, in case he should have forgotten anything. Why save any of this, when its only function could be to make problems in the future? Why not burn all of it? Those forgotten, torn-edged letters, curled and silent. (Neat letters, elegant and aloof. Letters of blue ink, set down rapidly. Letters which suggest a sort of urgency, a sort of compulsion. Letters which hold implication, which invite examination. Letters which seem to promise the answer to some question and then begin to suggest the darkening of a thought, the casting of an idea like a shadow. Letters which seem to push towards the light, but then send their roots deeper. Letters which begin to enfold and seem at first warm but then a little cooler, which seem to be there and yet dissolve into something else, and the bridge between the seen and the unseen, between the known and the unknown and the connections, growing like the healing of a wound, like the clotting of blood or the callousing of worn skin. Letters matted into layers, into strata; layers which seem meaningless and yet have the weight of another's guilt, and which bring neither a warning nor a threat but only the confirmation of something previously suspected, and gradually the forming of a pattern, a hierarchy, and the sense that each layer, each letter of blue ink is not an answer complete in itself but only an indication, a hint, a point where things meet, a point of confluence, of ramification, and each letter, curled and silent, bears witness to a crime and the idea of a crime, and an act of intrusion.)

Lifting out the past, in all its torn and forgotten pieces. And then he saw it – lying in its bed of paper; across the heap of envelopes, newly unearthed. A hair; a long strand of brown hair. Jenny's. And King felt sick with dread.

He picked it up, held the hair between his fingers; studied it closely. It couldn't be anyone's, but hers. And it had been lying deep within the pile of papers.

This still proved nothing, except that Jenny might have opened this drawer. Or the hair could have been on King's clothes, or blown into the drawer while he was rummaging in it. The strand of hair proved nothing.

Yet it was here. It was lying hidden in a heap of envelopes. He tried to imagine this hair on the head of every woman who had ever slept in this room. But it could only be Jenny's.

The drawer pulled out, tipped over; everything spread on the floor. Frantic searching – for what? For what might already have been removed?

All of it, in the metal waste paper bin; he could burn it a handful at a time. What is the past, except the possibility of accusation? But even the first handful – so much smoke. He opened the window again, but it was scarcely sufficient. To go outside, though, might look suspicious. A room smelling of smoke now, and a bin full of charred paper – larger pieces still bearing the possibility of some degree of decipherment. Ground finer. Difficult to destroy everything. He went through what was left – all those old letters, notes, bills, cards. Nothing that could do any harm now if a stranger found it. He put it all in a bag and took it outside to the dustbin. When he went back, the room still smelled of smoke, and he felt foolish and resentful.

But he could not forget the hair. It was not what he had found that he feared, but what he had not found.

Next day, he woke early. Once in his office, he was quite unable to work. He spent the morning hoping for news from Robert that might make everything alright. Or even from Jenny. Again and again, he tried to reassure himself of the triviality of his wrong-doing; he was fearful only of this uncertainty, this silence and expectation.

When lunchtime came, he felt only slightly calmer. He went home as usual and sat down at the piano.

19

Later that afternoon, King returned to his office. Joanna called out to him as he passed her room. Someone had been looking for him. Charles asked who it was – she didn't know; he wouldn't give a name. Only said he'd return later.

King found it impossible to do any work. He tried reading a paper, but he only scanned the equations without following anything of what was going on. Then the phone rang, and Joanna put Jenny through to him. Jenny said it had been a lovely weekend. Her voice sounded as if she were thinking of something else.

'And you know what, Charles? I've still got your spare key – I forgot to leave it yesterday. You don't need it do you?'

Charles felt again that fearful sensation of vulnerability.

'No. It's alright. I'll come down to London at the weekend. I can get it from you then.'

Jenny hesitated in answering.

'You're sure you want to come? I could always post it to you.'

'Why shouldn't I want to come?'

'Look, Charles, I don't understand what's going on. But maybe we both need to stop a while and think things over.'

Now it was Charles who paused.

'Perhaps you're right. I'll talk to you later in the week.'

It was as if there were some barrier between them. Eventually he would have no choice but to confront her, and find out the truth. Reason enough in itself, perhaps, for going to London to see her. But he still needed time.

Impossible to work. Symbols swam without meaning before his eyes. He went to Joanna's office.

'What was he like – this man who was looking for me?'

'Seemed a bit nervous. Wouldn't tell me anything.'

'How old?'

'Early thirties. Appallingly dressed!' Joanna laughed, and carried on arranging the papers on her desk.

'How was he dressed?'

'Looked like two halves of different suits. And dreadful shoes.'

'Sounds like you got a good look at him.'

'Women notice these things, Charles. I don't think he was anything to get too excited about. Looked to me like a physicist. I expect he'll be back.'

To Joanna, it was little more than a source of amusement. Charles resented her lack of concern about the stranger.

'We can't have just anyone wandering around the place, Joanna. That's how things go missing.'

Impossible to work. Sitting at his desk, he tried to begin a calculation. Still the thought of that hair was in his mind; that strand of Jenny's hair amongst his papers. He picked up the phone and dialled Robert's work number. There was no reply. No better when he tried Robert's home.

He went upstairs to the tea-room. Perhaps a newspaper would provide some distraction. Going in, he noticed a man sitting in a corner of the room. Dark, greasy hair – and matching Joanna's unfavourable description. Sitting alone, apparently in deep thought. If he saw King, he had ignored him.

King took a newspaper from the rack and chose a good seat from which to observe the stranger. It was conceivable that he was a physicist, come to discuss something or other. Too conspicuous and odd, surely, to be with the police. His battered briefcase didn't look very official. And they must have better things to do than sit in tea-rooms all day.

King noisily turned a few pages while watching discreetly. No use avoiding it – if this was the one who had come to King's office then he would try again sooner or later. Better to get it over with. King got to his feet, walked up to him and introduced himself.

'Ah, Dr. King – I'm most honoured to meet you.' A bony hand was extended. 'My name is Edward Warren.'

King gave a sigh. So it was only that madman who had sent him his 'Vision of the Universe'.

'I was hoping you could spare me some of your valuable time to discuss my ideas – if it isn't too inconvenient.'

Not at all, King told him, and he led him back downstairs to his office. Warren followed in silence.

'Take a seat please, Mr. Warren.' Perhaps this was the kind of distraction Charles needed. It shouldn't take long to get rid of him.

Warren sat stiffly, with his knees together – his heels clear of the floor. He reached for his briefcase, and pulled out some papers which he handed to King. 'A Vision of the Universe: Addendum'.

'These are some further results – I didn't want to rewrite the whole thing until I had your comments.'

Charles perched on the edge of his desk and looked down at the strange figure. 'Thanks very much for sending them to me, Mr. Warren.'

'My pleasure. Was I right to use those margins? I know they should be wide, but I didn't want to overdo it.'

'The margins? Oh, they're fine. It's what's in between that I'm not so sure about.'

'I appreciate, Dr. King, that the ideon theory is perhaps a little difficult to take in in its entirety at a first reading. It is, after all, the result of many years of work.'

'I'm sure. I admire your energy.' Now King had found Warren's opus beneath some other papers on the desk. He picked it up, and began to leaf through it. 'You say you want to publish this?'

'Not only want – I regard it as a sacred duty.'

'Well, you must understand that I can't really help you on that one. I can give you the addresses of some journals . . .'

'I have them already, Dr. King. I'm not stupid. But none of them is suitable for work like this.'

'Ah, I'm glad you appreciate that.'

'You see, they have my name now, and they are under instructions not to publish anything by me. The ideon theory would show them all up for the shin-barking cretins that they are; they can't afford to admit the truth of my ideas. Even if I were to submit my work under a pseudonym, they would know that I was behind it; the ideon theory is so inextricably linked with the name of Edward Warren, they would see at once through such a plan.'

'So what do you want me to do?'

'Dr. King, a revolution is approaching in the world of physics. Who can say who will be its heroes, its victims? Its martyrs? But this revolution cannot be started by a single man, no matter how great his vision. He needs allies, helpers. Dr. King, I want you to be my ally.'

King shifted on the edge of his desk, and rubbed his chin. 'I see. So really the best thing would be for me to give you my honest opinion of your theory?'

'I humbly beseech it of you. I have come to seek your judgement.'

King opened the 'Vision' at page one. 'Very well. Let's take your opening chapter, "The speed of light is not constant". I have to disagree with you on that one.'

'You disagree?' Warren laughed. 'But Dr. King, how can you too miss such a blindingly simple proof; how do you explain the action of a lens?'

'You're right, the light slows down when it passes through a lens. It's the speed of light in a vacuum that's constant. There are very good theoretical reasons, and there's no evidence to the contrary.'

Warren got to his feet, and put his hands through his greasy hair. He began to pace up and down in the small office, so that King had to move from his place on the edge of the desk, and stand clear of the troubled figure. 'Nonsense – shameful nonsense! Dr. King, I thought better of you, I truly thought that you of all people might have the vision, the courage, the will to join me in my struggle. I thought that you at least would have in you the spirit of the revolutionary.'

King flinched. 'What makes you think that? Why should

I be any more revolutionary than all the other physicists you could have contacted?'

Warren ignored him. 'I can see they've already had you in for mind-control, the thought engineers at the Academy of Science. I suppose you don't remember anything about it, do you? They always give you something to take away the memory afterwards. Don't you see, they've blinded you! You say you're a man of science, and a seeker of the truth – you're nothing more than another instrument of propaganda for Zionist science. Now you're going to tell me all this rubbish about time dilation and E equals mc squared. You've been duped, Dr. King, like all the others. I've come here to make you free, and all you can do is tell me this magic formula, that the speed of light is constant.'

King spoke quietly. 'Why did you send your work to me?'

'Because I thought that you of all people would be a believer in truth, freedom, justice . . .'

'But why?' King had to hold himself back from shaking Warren's thin body between his hands. 'Why should I be the one who might care about truth and freedom? Where did you get my name from?'

Warren could see that he was now beginning to make some impression, and this gladdened him. 'You are a lover of truth, Dr. King. You won't deny me that, will you? One who will champion the divine right of science to overcome all lies and deception – to conquer the dictatorship of ignorance?'

King was feeling increasingly uneasy. Why should Warren have chosen him as the champion of liberty? Might he even know something about Flood? By now, King was prepared to suspect absolutely anyone. 'All scientists believe in truth, Mr. Warren – whatever truth means. But tell me what gave you the idea that I could be of any help to you. Who gave you my name? What did they say about me?'

Warren was standing by the window now, looking out. 'You and I, Dr. King – we could take them all on. You're

149

a respected scientist; you know the right people – you've got all the contacts. A good word from you, that's all it would take. I don't expect my theory to be accepted overnight, of course. When an idea is so original and ahead of its time, naturally it takes a while for the rest of humanity to catch up. But they must catch up.' He turned and approached King. 'Humanity must be made to understand its blind folly – the eyes of the world must be opened to the pernicious ideology of relativity; this anti-Christian, idolatrous, obscene collection of lies.'

King sat down on the chair which Warren had abandoned, and looked up at the strange, crazed figure in his two halves of different suits. 'I'm not going to help you, Mr. Warren. Perhaps I've been duped, but I disagree with your theory. I think it's all nonsense. Maybe you're right and I'm mistaken, but you've got your beliefs and I've got mine, and we'll have to agree to differ. I'd just like to know who suggested you send your work to me.'

'Maybe you're mistaken?' Warren stared at King in disbelief. 'How calmly the fool admits his ignorance! Maybe indeed. You don't even care either way, do you? What difference does it make, if all your physics is a load of cosmic bollocks – you've got your cosy office with a nice big desk. Who cares if it's all rubbish?' Again Warren was reaching for his shiny hair. 'God, you make me sick. You don't even have to justify yourselves; rejecting everything out of hand. Not even prepared to debate the issue like a gentleman.'

King had tired of this nonsense. He stood up. 'Very well, if it'll make you happy, then let's go through the whole damn lot and I'll tell you what I think of it. But first, just tell me one thing, Mr. Warren. Why the hell did you come to me? What help was I supposed to be able to give you?'

Warren sneered, and muttered something – possibly in Latin. 'The thought engineers must have done a fine job on you. I expected better. I knew that someone here had to be my chosen helper; I thought I had interpreted the signs correctly, but I can see I was mistaken.'

'What signs?' King was becoming more and more suspicious of this lunatic. He should have left his office door open.

'A line sent to me in the newspaper: *He is a born leader.* I had to find a born leader, to help me in the struggle. I checked the names of the staff here a few weeks ago, on the board at the entrance, and there I saw it: King. Leader of men.'

Charles gave a barely suppressed groan as he took his place again on the edge of the desk. 'I've got ten minutes, Mr. Warren. I'm going to spend them explaining why I think you're wrong. Then I have to go somewhere else. Now please sit down.'

King began to talk about Maxwell's equations, about clocks and light signals, and the bending of starlight round the sun during a total eclipse. He could see that Warren accepted none of it.

'Dr. King, you're nothing but a blind fool. You start from the assumption that the velocity of light is the greatest speed, and you eventually use it to prove precisely the same thing. I've heard it all before – it's a circular argument! The rabbis at the Academy of Science did a fine job on you, oh yes.' Warren got to his feet. 'I came to free you, and yet you choose enslavement.' Then without warning he lunged at King, who grabbed him by the jacket and easily threw him back against the wall, which he hit with a loud bang. A most undignified scene.

The door opened – it was Joanna, come to see what all the noise was about.

'Phone security,' King told her, 'and have them escort this man out of the building.'

'No need for that,' said Warren. 'I'm going – no point wasting my breath here any longer. You're a fool, King. A blind fool. You'll see.' And with that, he left.

Charles and Joanna stared at each other in bewildered silence. She brought out a paper handkerchief. 'Are you alright? I think he scratched your face.' He took it from her, and wiped the sweat from his brow.

Others were in the corridor, looking round the door, trying to see what was going on. King told them it was all over. He only wanted to be left alone. He would have preferred it if no-one had seen him like this. Especially Joanna.

He went home early. It had been a strange and disturbing day – the distraction of Warren serving only to leave him feeling even more uneasy. His suspicions concerning Jenny, and his fears about what might happen next, still had not left him. He rang Robert – this time he found him in.

'Charles? What a surprise.'

Some kind of forced humour. Robert's voice sounded strained and unnatural. He might have been drinking.

'Heard any more, Robert – about anything?'

'Actually, very busy at the moment, Charles, can't talk. Lot of work to get through. Things to sort out. I'll ring you back.'

'I need to see you, Robert. I think you were right. About Jenny.'

'Really tied up at the moment Charles. Not a good idea to see you. Things are in a bit of a mess. I'll ring. Bye now.'

The following morning, Joanna told King she was sorry about the unfortunate incident with Warren; she felt somehow responsible. He said it was best forgotten. He put the 'Vision of the Universe' in the bin. Shortly before lunchtime, the phone rang.

'Dr. King? This is Inspector Mays here – central Cambridge police station. Wondered if you could come down and see us for a quick word. Just some routine stuff. Nothing to get alarmed about.'

20

'Take a seat, Dr. King. Tell me, how long have you known Robert Waters?'

'About five years. We met once in a cafe, and got talking. Found we had a lot in common. We've remained friends ever since.'

'Did he tell you that we asked him to come here last week?'

'Ah, no. I don't think so.'

'You don't think so?'

'No. Should he have?'

'No reason why he shouldn't. Word "Flood" mean anything to you?'

'Yes – why? Is there one on the way?'

'No, I mean as the name of something. Are you sure Waters never mentioned it, or said anything about things he'd written – essays or poems?'

'Quite sure.'

'We can come back to it later. But have a look at this document, now. Do you recognize it?'

'Of course. It's my latest paper.'

'Did you type it yourself?'

'No, a friend did it. Jenny Lindsay.'

'Is she your girlfriend? What's her address?'

'Flat 9, 34 Owen Terrace, Bayswater.'

'Did she type it in London?'

'No, here.'

'Comes to see you often, does she?'

'No, I usually see her in London.'

'Got any other girlfriends?'

'Is that important?'

'Could be. Have you got any other girlfriends?'

'No.'

'Happy enough with the one. That's nice. Surprised you aren't married, nice looking chap at your age. Good job. Good education. Not the marrying type, eh?'

'Maybe one day.'

'Do you sleep with her?'

'Look, what is all this about?'

'Well, it sounds like you're sleeping at an address in London every weekend. Have you informed the Housing Office about that?'

'It's never more than two nights, and it isn't every weekend anyway.'

'If you make a habit of staying for three, you know you need to tell the Housing Office.'

'Yes, I know.'

'Are you a homosexual, Dr. King.'

'No. What sort of a question is that?'

'A relevant one, to our enquiry. Eligible man like you, still single.'

'But I told you, I've got a girlfriend.'

'Do you sleep with her?'

'Yes.'

'Do you like it?'

'What's this got to do with your enquiry?'

'Maybe you're really a queer but you haven't found out yet. Or haven't admitted it to yourself.'

'Yes I enjoy sleeping with her.'

'And does she enjoy it?'

'You'd have to ask her that.'

'Perhaps we will. All in good time. Now, Dr. King, this paper of yours. When your girlfriend typed it, whose typewriter did she use?'

'I borrowed one from Robert.'

'Robert Waters? That's very interesting.'

'What do you mean?'

'Well, take a look at this other document now, Dr. King – ever seen it before? Nothing very important, just an old pamphlet that was made a few years ago by some discontent would-be intellectual. Worth six months at the outside, or maybe a fine. Have a good look at it. Notice anything?'

'It's called Flood.'

'But do you notice anything else? Look at the capital F.

See how it goes a bit faint in the middle, so there's almost a gap? Does it all the way through, every time it's typed. Now let's compare it with your paper. See, the word 'For' – it's the same F, isn't it? Your paper and Flood were typed on the same machine.'

'So what does this prove?'

'That your friend Robert Waters wrote Flood.'

'I see. And why are you telling me all this?'

'Why? To see if you disagree. You're a very logical man, Dr. King. So use a bit of logic, now. What have we proved?'

'You've proved that my paper and Flood were typed on the same machine.'

'Therefore?'

'Therefore . . . nothing. Somebody borrowed Robert's typewriter to write Flood.'

'Yes . . . sounds reasonable. But then Waters must know who wrote it.'

'In that case you should talk to him.'

'We already have, Dr. King. Remember? We've interviewed him twice. He's being vetted for some government work – I expect he told you about it. And we asked him about Flood. Know what he said? He said he'd never heard of it. What do you make of that?'

'Did you show him my paper?'

'We hadn't seen it yet, then. But now that we have, it changes things, doesn't it? More or less clears the matter up.'

'But one of his friends could have asked to borrow the typewriter on any pretext.'

'Like typing a paper, for example?'

'I told you, I had nothing to do with it.'

'And I'm prepared to believe you. We got the Office of Publications to send us all your papers, and this is the only one that's been done using Waters' typewriter. So I'd say you're in the clear. For the moment.

'Look, Dr. King, ordinarily I couldn't give a monkey's about stuff like this; old pamphlets – poetry, for Christ's sake. My job is catching criminals. But Waters is being vetted for a responsible job. And it's not just the fact that he might have written this shit that I'm worried about. Did you know he's a pouf?'

'Is he?'

'You mean he's never told you? Never made a pass at you? Nice looking chap like you? Waters is queer, and I've got as much proof as I could want.'

'In that case, I don't see how I can be of any more help to you.'

'Oh, but you can. This is only the start of the enquiry, believe me. Look, they want Waters to do some book; we tell them he might be a security risk. But they say he's the only man for the job, so we've just got to keep an eye on him. And that's where you come in.'

'Me?'

'I want you to keep an eye on him. You say he's your friend, Dr. King, but it sounds like you hardly even know him – what he really is. He's a subversive and a homosexual. Not the sort I'd want for a friend of mine. I want you to talk to him. Let him confide in you. I want to know who all his other pouf friends are. Maybe some of them were doing this Flood business.'

'So all of this is about catching homosexuals? Robert is my friend – do you really expect me to spy on him? Even if I said I'd do it, I could easily make it all up if I wanted.'

'You could. But that would be a very silly thing to do. And maybe our enquiry would turn up something on you. Something you didn't even know you'd done. Please, Dr. King, don't fuck around with us. I know you're in this more than you're letting on, but for the time being I don't really care. It's Waters I'm after. Him and his fairies. Try covering up for them and I might start wondering again if you're one as well. Just get me a name. A name for starters. You'll find it gets easier as you go along.'

'But why? Why all this, simply to catch a man out? You bring me in here, you talk about my paper – what made you connect the paper with Flood? That's what brought it all out about Robert, isn't it? What's Jenny been saying? She's one of your spies, isn't she?'

'Jenny? Your girl? Yes, maybe you should keep an eye on her as well. Can't trust anyone these days. Just get me some names, Dr. King – it's not much to ask. You'll be doing the world a favour. And yourself.'

'How can you possibly expect me to betray my own friend?'

'How? Well, it seems to me you're not really in any position to refuse. You see, it's like this. One day we get instructions from Section Five to check Waters out. So the first thing I do is send two men to do a routine search of his office in the university. Nothing heavy, just the usual once over. Do the drawers, a quick gander at the shelves – see if he's reading anything dodgy. And check a few books in case there's something hidden between the pages. One of my men takes a book – picks it at random – then taps the edge of it on the table. And a little piece of paper drops out – just a scrap, that's been torn off a sheet and written on. Doesn't seem anything special, but he brings it back just in case. Look, I've got it here. See? Read for yourself: FLO 343592. The number look familiar? That's right; it's your phone number. No problem for us to check that out. But what could FLO mean? I decide to have a look through the files just in case, and what should I happen to turn up but Flood, this old pamphlet here. Waters/Flood – get it? Some rubbish in it about history – sort of thing he knows about. But not only that, there's all this poetry. Horrible pouf stuff. Hardly Wordsworth, I can tell you. And then this other article – all about making queers legal. Gives us some idea of the kind of man he is. A subversive and a homosexual. Charming friends you've got, Dr. King.

'So now we've got the whole story. Waters is putting together this pamphlet. He meets you in a cafe and you get talking. He reckons you might be willing to help him, and he wants to take your number, so he looks in his pockets or his bag for a scrap of paper. Later he rings you, and you meet somewhere more private where he tells you what he's doing.'

'No. No, that's not true.'

'Then he sticks this bit of paper in a book and forgets all about it until my man comes along five years later.'

'I can't believe Robert would do anything like this.'

'You mean he never said anything to you about Flood?'

'Never.'

'In that case, can you tell me why he wrote those letters beside your phone number?'

'I don't know . . . We arranged to meet. To play music together. The letters must have been some kind of short-hand – an abbreviation perhaps. They could have meant anything. What is there to connect them with that pamphlet; just because there's something in it about history?'

'No point trying to cover up for him. Remember, Flood was done on his typewriter.'

'But you didn't know about that until today! What made you so sure already about Flood? Christ, it is Jenny isn't it?'

'Let's just call it copper's intuition. Look, I know that you were involved in all this stuff somehow – but it doesn't really matter. Not as long as I can have Waters. Just give me what I want, and you can go on doing your physics in peace. I want one rat to lead me to other rats. This Flood business – I'm fucking sick of it; this is nothing. But your friend Waters is a very nasty piece of work, and I'm going to have him. Him and all his anti-social friends. Just get me a name for starters, then you can go free. But try fucking us around and believe me, we can make your comfortable little life extremely difficult. Do I make myself clear? Now Perkins'll show you out. Try and get me something by next week.'

21

Five years earlier, Robert Waters would bring his violin once or twice a week to Charles King's house, where they would play music together. During the second such meeting, King mentioned again his ideas for Flood, and he was surprised that Robert now seemed far more enthusiastic about it. Again, Robert had brought the folder of poems he had written, but this time he was prepared to let Charles read some of the contents.

A few days previously, King had told Anne that he wanted to end their affair. They had met after she finished work; Charles waited for her outside the school, and watched the clumps of children hurrying out at the end of the day. She had told him to go inside to meet her, nevertheless he preferred to wait. It was a cold winter's afternoon, but the idea of going into the school seemed to him somehow ridiculous. When eventually she came out she kissed him on the cheek, and they took a walk together by the river. This was when he told her that he wanted to end things.

It was unusual for Charles to terminate a relationship in this way. His attitude was that once you have slept with a woman, then something has come into being which never ends; some hidden thing – even though you might never see her again, you know that whenever you do there will still exist that mysterious, unspoken agreement which the meeting of flesh – however brief – necessarily implies. Relationships, as far as Charles was concerned, although they could change, could no more be ended than could a memory. But it was easy, perhaps, for him to feel this way, since the bond that held him to any particular woman was always a weak and tenuous thing. He had slept with Anne out of a curiosity that was aroused one afternoon in a museum, and now his curiosity was satisfied. One day his memory of her would be more vague, and he would feel

159

interested again. In the meantime it was better to stop. But he could see that she felt differently; that she was becoming attached to him, and wanted things that he couldn't give, and this had made him begin to feel resentful. The situation had to be dealt with now, before it got out of hand.

Charles and Robert went through that Mozart sonata again; the one which they had first played together the previous week. Afterwards they had tea as before. Already they were forming a ritual, and this was only the second time they had come together like this. How easy it is for habits to form. King told Robert he had finished his essay, The River of History, and was eager to show it to him.

Robert said he found it 'interesting', which Charles knew to be a sign of disapproval. 'History is about people, Charles. It's not some kind of equation.'

Charles said he wanted to see history as an abstract process – rather like the evolution of different species. He imagined a sort of natural selection of ideas. Then he started talking about mountains and potential surfaces, and history as some kind of minimizing of free energy, and Robert was completely lost.

'History ought to be all about the increase of human freedom,' said Robert, 'but it clearly isn't. History is a gradual accumulation of human misery.'

King was walking with Anne beside the river. Already the afternoon light was fading. He told her that he wouldn't be able to see her much during the next few weeks – because he was very busy at work.

This was the best he could do! The nation was in a state of upheaval; people were talking about change at last – perhaps even revolution. And Charles was agonizing over how to explain to Anne that her body no longer held for him that fascination he had felt when he watched her in the museum a few weeks earlier. How to tell her without hurting her feelings? King was writing essays about the need to seize the moment, to stand up and join the great tide of human will. And he was walking beside a river with a woman whose emotions frightened him.

They played some more music – a Beethoven sonata,

and then Robert put his hand on King's shoulder, and suggested they stop again for a while. Last week he had done the same, but now the hand rested longer. Last week, Robert had made such a gesture, and Charles had permitted it. And permission was given for this further, more sustained gesture which was now being presented.

Robert brought out some of his writing – from his briefcase, he drew that folder which King had found last week among the pile of scores. There had been time now to make a few improvements – perhaps some of it could go in King's proposed pamphlet. He handed him a sheet to read – a translation from the Greek poet Cavafy. It was a fair copy written in Robert's neat hand. Was his decision to show this to Charles another gesture?

One a.m. it must have been,
or half past one.
                    In a corner of the old taverna;
behind the wooden partition.
Except for the two of us, the shop completely empty.
A single oil lamp barely lighting it.
At the door, the faithful waiter nodding off.

Nobody would see us. Though already
we were so aroused,
we'd gone beyond all thought of caution.

Clothes half opened – few anyway,
in the divine heat of July.

Pleasure of flesh between
half-opened clothes;
Brief nakedness of flesh – an idea which has
travelled through twenty-six years and now
has settled in this poetry.

King was rereading the last verse, and he was thinking of Anne's flesh – that delight of first seeing, first touching, which could never be recaptured. What memories would one day come to him across a space of years?

Robert sat close beside him, and reached out to take back the page which King held. Robert's hand close to King's, together on the page. Then King released his hold on the paper. He asked Robert about the poet, Cavafy. Robert said he had the original Greek text with him; he reached into his briefcase and brought out a small brown-covered book. Strange, King thought, that he should have carried this book with him; perhaps with the specific intention of showing it as part of an explanation. Last week, Robert had begged King not to look at his work; now, he had had time to plan its presentation.

Robert opened the book at the appropriate page and handed it to Charles, who now tried to follow the Greek symbols which always reminded him of mathematics. Easy to forget that this really was somebody's language. He only knew ancient Greek – and had forgotten most of that – and he could make no sense of the text before him. He admired Robert's skill. He handed it back, and asked to see other translations.

Robert opened the folder again and brought out some more pages. Again the closeness of shared reading; shared holding of the flimsy sheets. Poems about classical history, or memories of young Greek men. And then at last another sheet – more like a working draft now, with rough scribbles and words crossed out and corrected.

'This is one of my own,' said Robert.

> In a cafe, once more I heard
> Your voice – those sparse and frugal notes.
> Do they not say that you spoke your native Greek
> With an English accent?
>
> Briefest of visions: eyes meet across the cafe;
> A man of about my age – eyelids heavy,
> Perhaps from recent pleasures.
> I begin the most innocent of conversations.
>
> Again I see that image;
> Ancient delight of flesh

Against guiltless flesh.
Sweeter still, in its remembering.

Most innocent of conversations: once more, I am mistaken.
He leaves; the moment lost – and to forgo
The squalor of this place, I read again your lines;
   those sparse and frugal notes.
In a taverna, you found beauty, long ago.

And when you draw, with your slim, swift pen
The image of that memory – time's patient hostage;
Then how can I forget him, that boy
   whom you could not forget,
Or that music, in a foreign language?

   Reading it twice over, King asked himself how he should respond to this gesture. He read again some of the lines, and thought of that first meeting two weeks earlier, and he asked himself if he were the man whom Robert had written about. Still, Robert was sitting close beside him, waiting for some reaction. And then King felt the approach once more of Robert's hand; his hand on the page, close to King's – not attempting to take away the paper. And a finger of Robert's hand extended, and reaching out towards King's. A silent question.
   (They were walking by the river, the two of them. Anne, trying to understand King's meaning. They would still be friends, of course. And once he knew he had hurt her, further hurt became easier.)
   Charles let go of the page, stood up, moved away from Robert. Robert lowered his head in apology. Charles searched for words. He said they'd better forget all about it.
   And then the doorbell sounded. Charles went to answer while Robert hastily drew together his handwritten sheets. It was Anne. King thought she looked as if she had been crying, but she said she was alright.
   Entering the flat, Anne would have had the feeling that she was interrupting something; Robert, that it might be

best for him to leave. But King was glad that she was here. He made the necessary introductions, and the three entered into a superficial conversation.

Each was grateful for the lightness which the presence of a third person now permitted. Anne forgot the tears she had shed, and had been afraid of renewing. Robert felt saved from humiliation. And King was relieved of the sense of vulnerability by which he had been seized. They made the most superficial of conversations. King offered to make more tea.

Anne and Robert got on well together, and soon Robert was talking freely with her about his work; she said she found history fascinating. Robert spoke easily, while King remained quieter. They were talking about their backgrounds, their families – things which King had never asked about. Watching Anne as she spoke and moved her hands, King rediscovered something of the fascination which had drawn him to her. As he watched Anne, he sensed that Robert was watching him.

Robert was under the impression that Anne and Charles were in love – which was possibly half true. Perhaps he saw Anne as a way into Charles's heart. In any event, they were soon to become intimate friends.

When she had entered the flat, Anne looked tired and drawn. Now she had forgotten the excuse which brought her to the place; she was chatting amiably. And she too, while she talked to Robert, was watching Charles.

Why would Anne and Robert eventually come to sleep together? It may have been no more than the merging of two streams, which had run down from opposite slopes into a common valley.

Robert drew Charles back into the conversation, with mention of the music they had been practising together. Anne said she wanted to hear them play. Charles was reluctant – he insisted he wasn't as good as Robert made out. But Robert was already lifting his violin from its case, and checking the tuning, so Charles went to the piano stool.

Robert spoke to Anne. 'Why don't you turn the pages for Charles?' She said she couldn't read music, but Robert told her Charles would give a nod at the appropriate times.

The Beethoven sonatas were still on the music rack, and Robert suggested the Kreutzer. Charles felt, though didn't say, that it was a little unfair to choose a piece with such a difficult piano part – he would have preferred something simpler like the Spring. But then Robert began to play the opening bars, the sound of the unaccompanied violin filling the room and making every object within it seem to resonate. It was a piece which Robert had practised very thoroughly.

What would lead Anne and Robert eventually to sleep together? Revenge against Charles, perhaps? Theirs would be a relationship based on friendship rather than sex; on trust rather than curiosity.

Charles was beginning to play his part of the slow introduction. Anne sat close beside him on a chair she had pulled into position. He wondered if she would be in the way when he reached for the bass. Now the quickening of the tempo; the main movement. When Anne reached to turn the page, King could smell her perfume.

He would not waver in his earlier judgement. Watching Anne speak with Robert, he had felt again that thrill of desire – but it was only because she was giving her attention to someone else.

King was playing badly, but after the first mistake, the others became easier to tolerate. It was an effort to remember to make it clear to Anne when to turn the page. With his peripheral vision of her on his left, he could see that she mostly watched Robert. Was this perhaps some game on her part to arouse King's jealousy? Yet for him, the situation would be perfect – to be free of her, and yet to desire her. If she became Robert's lover, then he would truly want her. In the easier moments of the music, when King could find a brief period of relaxation, he imagined the joining of those two bodies; Anne's and Robert's – he pictured how they would look. Anne's body, all too easy to reconstruct in his mind, but still more interesting now beneath the shadow of another.

Charles knew Robert only through the performing of music, and he knew Anne only through the performing of sex. And with Robert, King was not afraid to play wrong notes. The two of them were beginning to laugh at the mistakes they were making. Anne remained silent, for fear of offending.

After the end of the first movement, Charles said they had better stop – his hands were tired, and his mind was not on the music. Anne told them they both played beautifully. She could still feel the distant memory of the shiver which had run through her body during those austere opening bars. Afterwards, she would remember how Robert looked as he drew the bow across the strings; the careless fall of his fringe, and the concentration in his eyes.

Was the union of Robert and Anne already ordained in those chords, and that remembered shiver?

22

By the end of the following week, Charles and Robert had produced Flood. King wanted Robert to write an essay about the oppression of homosexuals, but Robert was reluctant to do this. He said his poems expressed everything that he wanted to communicate on the subject. So Charles wrote it instead – 'A Plea for Tolerance'. Strangely, it was this essay, which he wrote quickly one evening, which was to lead to the events five years later which would change his life, and bring Robert's to an end. In fact, it was not even the essay itself – but rather a single sentence. Who would have thought, that a few words could have such effect?

The hypocrisy of the situation is nowhere more apparent than in the pronouncements of Cecil Grieve, whose own taste for young men is well known.

Robert had argued that the line should be dropped – that King was implicitly attacking what he was trying to defend. King said it was the hypocrisy he objected to, not Grieve's proclivities, and refused to make the cut. In fact, he was pleased with the opportunity the pamphlet gave him to attack a political figure for whom he had a particular contempt. Nor was Robert at all sympathetic to the man who had been so vigorous in the campaign for 'social morals', but he felt hurt by the attitude which King had revealed.

The line stayed. Robert typed the five pages of Flood – the two articles, two translated poems, and three of his own which he signed 'Ganymede'. Then King made clandestine use of the photocopier in the physics department to produce fifty copies. Some were placed in people's pigeonholes in the university, others surreptitiously slid between the pages of magazines in newspaper shops, or left behind in cafes. One found its way onto the noticeboard of the history department.

It was all little more than a prank – the sort of thing which everyone was doing during those three or four months when it seemed that the rules were no longer completely rigid, but could be subjected to a little bending. For King, it was simply a chance to feel that he was doing something. Robert, on the other hand, did his part with a sense of release and abandon. The copy in the history department survived for three days on the noticeboard – Robert stopped once to read it, admiring the poetry as if it were the work of another. He imagined his words being discussed by people he had never met – sympathetic souls who were out there somewhere, though he had no knowledge of them.

Within a few days, the pamphlet had been completely absorbed into the stream of human life – all copies were gone without trace. And that was the end of it, as far as King and Robert were concerned. They had the satisfaction of knowing that their efforts might perhaps have made some impression.

But it was that line, about Grieve, which was to lend to Flood its lasting influence. Without it, the pamphlet was illegal only because of the unauthorized way it had been produced and distributed - the contents of the essays and poems would never have got past the censor, of course; but in the atmosphere of liberality prevailing at that time they probably would not have been regarded as warranting any further action. But the line about Grieve raised it onto a new, far more illustrious level – the level of sedition. The copy which Robert admired on the notice board of the history department was sent by the relevant Party representative to the police, where it was put on file. And this was what Mays would find five years later, long after King had forgotten everything he had written.

How strange and ironic, that such a subtle difference can be so crucial! Like the poorly chosen phrase which can turn an intended compliment into an insult. How strange and ironic that a man should die because of a poor prank.

Charles and Robert continued their musical sessions,

though they became gradually less frequent. And Robert grew closer to Anne. At his suggestion, the three of them had begun to go out together – to films, or weekend excursions. Soon, King began to find excuses to make himself absent, and leave the other two in peace. When he was with Anne he felt a tension which he could do without.

It was Anne who eventually seduced Robert – in her grave and serious way, she reached the decision that it would be the right thing to do. They had already become firm friends – like brother and sister was how Robert described it. He had often been alone with her in her flat; neither had made any kind of move. One evening, Anne came and sat close to him, then kissed him firmly. He felt it would be impolite not to respond positively.

This was the gesture which led to a night of love making – tentative and uncertain at first, but then gradually less awkward, as fears and nervousness were overcome. It was a night which allowed Robert to convince himself that he was not after all doomed to a life of hopeless liaisons with members of his own sex – although he would subsequently find that he had been wrong in this conclusion. And Anne was gratified by the delicacy with which he treated her body; like a fragile flower to be studied and explored – not merely plucked and catalogued (which was Charles's way). It was only through this union with Robert that she came to realize how much resentment she felt against her former lover.

And yet she still found herself longing for him, in those early days when her affair with Robert was just beginning, and the one with Charles felt not quite over.

One evening she went to Charles's flat to return a book of his which had lain on her shelf. It was less than three months after that time when she had heard them both play the Kreutzer sonata, and her eyes had been heavy with tears held back. And it was three weeks after her first night with Robert. She felt ready now to seek some form of redress, and the book which she took to King's flat was nothing more than a pretext. She had come because she wanted King to know she no longer needed him.

And yet she ended up in King's bed. Was this what she had really wanted when she came to his flat?

He showed her in, and asked how she was, and Robert. He had seen less of him since the completion of Flood – about which King had said nothing to Anne, and he had assumed Robert would have done the same since to do otherwise would have meant compromising himself.

Something in Anne's reply – when she spoke about Robert – told King what the situation was; that they were now sleeping together. He saw again that vision which had appeared to him while accompanying Robert's violin; he saw her body – less familiar now, the memory becoming indistinct – shaded by that other figure. Would Robert have known what to do? King longed to ask.

He could see again that film of mystery which had covered her like a gauze, when he had first watched her lead a troop of schoolchildren round the museum. And he could sense that her apparent indifference to him – the ease with which she spoke – was only feigned. He had that special pleasure, of talking to a woman as if she were a comparative stranger, while savouring the memory of her body, and its particular forms, textures, odours.

He had no desire to speak about the past; it was Anne who brought it up. 'Can we forget it all now, and just be friends?'

'I already had forgotten it,' said King. He did not say this in order to hurt her. Even so, she was hurt – and King would not have minded if she had left at that moment.

'I do miss you sometimes,' she said. She was one of those women who try to cure an injury by laying themselves open to a further one. King told her that he also missed her, and they agreed that they had had good times together.

Then as the conversation continued, Anne said, 'You were very good for me, Charles – in a way. Sexually, I mean.'

If she had come to King's flat with an intention other than that of going to bed with him, then this comment was a mistake. Why had she made it?

When she first slept with Robert, she was impressed by his gentleness. Now already she had begun to wonder if this was really a symptom of a lack of interest on his part. Already she had had the feeling that when Robert was with her he was thinking of someone else. Which had in turn led her to let her mind wander elsewhere, towards other figures. The night before, while Robert made love to her, it was Charles who had been in her thoughts.

Charles now asked himself a question which had not previously seemed of any significance. Did he like Anne? When they were sleeping together, this was of no importance. But now she was proposing that they be friends – a much more serious matter. And the way that she had come here with a book as her excuse, in order to try and make him tell her that he missed her, made him wonder if there was something malign in her personality which should have been apparent to him earlier. He had the feeling she was flirting with him – perhaps this was because she knew no other way to behave. But he began to feel worried about what Robert might be letting himself in for.

She had come and sat down close beside him. She was asking how his work was going, and his piano playing, and whether he was seeing anyone else now.

King had not had sex for many weeks. The way that Anne had placed herself close beside him made him feel resentful. He reminded himself of how he had lain sleeping beside her body, its charms gone stale for him. Yet still he imagined that body, and the memory of it seemed far more interesting now. What was difficult to visualize, was how it was that he could have lain beside her nakedness and not have wanted to turn and embrace it. He felt resentful, yet aroused. These two sensations gnawed at each other like struggling creatures.

He began talking about Robert; what a fine musician he was. Anne agreed, but Charles could sense now that she was not in love with him. When she spoke about Robert, it was with a barely suppressed sigh. She admired him, liked him – clearly trusted him. And perhaps she had already decided that this was the man whom she should stay with. But Charles could tell that there was no real passion in her feelings for him.

'He's very good for you,' Charles said. 'I think he's the sort of man you needed.'

'What do you mean?' she moved away slightly from his side to look at him better. She drew her hair back behind her ear.

'Well, you seem a lot happier now.'

'I do?' By confirming what she had wanted to hear, Charles had now made her doubt the truth of it. Yes, she said – she was happier now.

She was sitting close enough for him to feel the pressure of her leg against his. She was wearing hideous blue slacks.

Charles felt he was being manipulated by her; the way she had placed herself beside him – and this conversation about past feelings, in which it was clear at every stage what she wanted him to say. If he were to put his hand now upon her leg, she would move away and tell him crossly to behave himself. Perhaps the sole purpose of her visit had been to give herself the opportunity of refusing him, just as he had refused her.

She seemed not to want to discuss Robert – always the conversation was brought back to things they had done together; she and Charles. He could smell her perfume, and he could taste both the mystery of their first encounter, and the irritation of this futile flirtation. She put her hand on his forearm as she talked. Soon it was his knee which was being subjected to brief taps with which she punctuated her speech.

At what point did King decide that a hand placed on her leg would not be removed by her? Thinking about it afterwards, he would realize that it was none of those mannered gestures of hers which had told him they would end up in bed together. Nor was it anything in what she was saying. But there was a moment, between words and gestures; a pause, when her mouth hung slightly open in hesitation, and he watched her open mouth and her eyes, and their heads were close enough for him to catch the unmistakably female scent of the breath she let out in that brief moment of silence. And then, once he knew that any advance made by him would not be repulsed, he became all the more determined not to make any. If a move was made, it would have to be by her.

This went on; the ballet of signs offered and declined, until at last Charles grew weary of it all. He looked at his watch – it was ten o'clock – then stood up and told her there were some papers he wanted to read before tomorrow. Anne said she had better go, but still she waited. Then spoke.

'Why did you really want to finish things between us, Charles?'

He turned and looked down at her. 'I never said I wanted to finish things. Only that I felt things had grown too stale for us to go on as we were.' He could see again that strangeness in her which had fascinated him once in the museum. She stood up, and moved to kiss him good-bye.

Which one was it who decided to prolong that kiss? If they had not both agreed to hold their lips each against the other's, then the kiss could not have been anything more than a peck. But it was a long embrace, sustained by old familiarity, and arms fell with ease into position – waists and shoulders reached for, held. Tongues long acquainted – most innocent of pleasures; a kiss which was no more than what had once been too trival for comment. A kiss which need have gone no further. Hands on thighs, and now on the borderline between flesh and clothing. Soon, the loosening and unbuttoning.

Then she stopped him – held him still in front of her. She said they should go to bed. And King reassured himself that he could not be betraying a friend for whom a woman's body could never be an object of sexual desire. As she lay beneath him and he went inside her, he thought of that time weeks before when the fingers of Robert's hand had reached across a page towards his. Innocent searching of fingers; innocent sliding of flesh against shared flesh.

It was a time of betrayal; a time which would be remembered for its lost hopes and abandoned dreams. A few days later, the so-called period of Consensus was brought to a sudden end. There were tanks on the streets, and pale faced young boys in ill-fitting uniforms stood with guns at the ready. The moment had been lost – the dam which King had written about had withstood the reservoir of discontent. Old sins were forgotten; new ones could take their place.

Some weeks passed – King saw nothing of Anne, and during the occasional musical sessions, Robert gave no indication that he might have found out what had taken place. Then one day when he arrived he seemed agitated. Anne was pregnant, and they were to be married.

King's first thought was that it must be his. But Robert didn't seem to suspect anyone else, and Charles was certainly not going to say anything to make him think otherwise. Robert's feelings were mixed – he spoke of his love for Anne, and his responsibility, and he even said he regarded it as a chance to make a 'fresh start'. He still believed that he would be able to put aside thoughts about other men.

At the wedding, King acted as witness. Anne maintained towards him a cold civility which would last until long after Robert's death, five years later. King congratulated her, kissed her lightly on the cheek. They exchanged pleasantries. Six months later, Duncan was born.

It was not long before Robert saw a young man who caught his eye, and he rediscovered the joy of the only natural act of physical love he knew. Others followed – some who broke his heart, and made him long to explain his feelings to the woman whom he loved as a sister. And furtive encounters which made him loathe his secrecy and his infidelity.

Charles also continued the familiar cycle of sexual exploration and disillusion. Meanwhile, the two men would meet now and again – to play music, or else simply to talk. Then one day, in London, Charles met a girl mending her bicycle, and she said her name was Jenny. And Robert told him that he had been chosen to write a book on the history of revolutions.

23

King's interview with Inspector Mays left him feeling frightened and confused. Mays knew that he and Robert had written Flood – but seemed not to be particularly interested in pursuing the matter. It was only an excuse to persecute Robert for his homosexuality; a means of blackmailing King into informing on his friend.

That night, King tried to decide what course of action he should take. Of course he wasn't going to betray Robert; but he had to satisfy the police somehow. Simple deceit would easily be seen through – and if he were to try and give some kind of warning, then how could he be sure the police wouldn't find out about it?

What was at stake? The worst they could do to King would be to prosecute him for his part in Flood. Six months, perhaps – or even a fine. For Robert, the situation was considerably worse – as he himself had said, when he had come to King's flat the Sunday before last to tell him about the book, and the search (little more than a week ago!) – as Robert had said; he risked losing his job, his marriage – not to mention five years in prison.

In the end, King could only see one course of action. He would do nothing. Faced with such an impossible dilemma, he felt like a hedgehog which runs neither one way nor the other, but curls itself into a ball and trusts to its spines. He would avoid Robert; if he saw him, he would say nothing – no use trying to warn him; Robert knew already what the danger was.

And Jenny? She had to be involved – why was that strand of her hair buried amongst his papers? There was no way that Flood could have been linked either to himself or to Robert, unless someone had given information to the police. The word FLO on a scrap of paper – what did that prove? There was Robert's typewriter, but that only gave Mays confirmation of what he had already known.

He would go and see Jenny at the weekend. As well for him in any case to stay away from Cambridge as much as he could, until things calmed down. Perhaps he would take a holiday somewhere.

It was only Tuesday evening; the time until the weekend, when he might at least discover what was going on, seemed unending. Work was impossible under such conditions.

On Thursday, Joanna came into his office and asked him if that madman had been back.

'Warren? No, I don't think we'll see him again. He's more of a danger to himself than to anyone else.'

Charles was sitting at his desk; Joanna had half-perched herself on it, close beside him. His eyes naturally directed themselves to her legs.

'They're the ones you gave me – the stockings. Nice, aren't they?' She had glanced at the open door, to see that the corridor was clear, before stretching a leg to show him the stocking. 'I still owe you one for these. I won't forget.'

Another cycle was beginning in Charles's life. Before long, he would sleep with Joanna.

There was no word from Robert, which for King was a relief. On Friday morning, King phoned Jenny at work and told her he would come to London tomorrow. It was a strained conversation; yes, there were some things they needed to discuss. And he had to get his spare key back from her.

Next morning, he took the train to London for his last visit to that small flat in Bayswater. It was less than ten weeks since he had first seen her in the Mall, mending her bicycle. Still not difficult to recapture the thrill of that promising wedge of cleavage beneath her low-hanging blouse.

There was a moment of forced good humour when he entered; they embraced. She was a stranger to him now. He could think only of that strand of her hair – he was studying her head; yes, the strand he found was certainly hers. And a hair fallen loose now on her shoulder. He picked it off with his fingers, and she looked at him quizzically. He smiled.

She went to finish washing some dishes – an attempt to make herself more relaxed. King looked round the flat and reminded himself of that miniature parody of domesticity – like the playhouse of a schoolgirl. But Jenny was not a schoolgirl.

He pulled back the flowered curtain which hid the bed; as he sat down on it, it creaked like an old pram. She came back from the tiny kitchen, and sat down beside him. Neither knew what to say, and so they began to kiss, mechanically. And like beings without will, they began to pull at each other's clothes, then position themselves on the bed, she drawing him on top of her. She was a stranger to him now.

They were two parts come together in an experiment. Two soulless chemicals merging, tumbling, to settle later into immiscible layers. There was a shelf on which stood two jars; one marked 'love' and the other 'betrayal', and they were being emptied over their bodies – wholly naked now; the bed creaking. Other chemicals: 'fear' and 'desire'; all thrown carelessly over them – their bodies wet with sweat. Holding her head and soft hair between his hands as he pushed himself into her, King rehearsed in his mind the scene in which he would learn the truth. How to obtain all the information he could, without making her realize he already knew what she must have done?

Their bodies colliding, struggling against an unseen force; that single force comprising good and evil, will and desire – their bodies pushing and pulling, and Jenny's eyes closed tightly – her face contorting as if in pain. But then it subsided, and was gone. And after a while, they struggled no more.

He withdrew, and lay on his back beside her. She asked if he was okay, and he said yes. He spoke quietly, while he stared at the ceiling – the only part of the bedsit that Jenny couldn't clean, since it was beyond reach. The only part that had no place in the playhouse of a little schoolgirl. It

178

looked like it could be the ceiling of a far more squalid room than this.

She was stroking his face, his chest, his shoulder. What was wrong? she asked. Nothing, he told her. Still, he hadn't completed his mental rehearsal. No way that he could think of, to be subtle about it.

'I've had a lot of things on my mind lately,' he said. She asked him if he wanted to talk about it. There was a worried note in her voice. Not now, he said.

She stood up and walked naked to the edge of the window – he watched the curve of her spine; the way it flowed from the neck down to the line of her buttocks. She stood at the edge of the window-frame, looking out across rooftops and grey clouds. 'Are you seeing someone else?' she said. He told her no, but felt he might sound insincere. So difficult to sound as if you're telling the truth sometimes, even when you really are.

'You can be honest with me Charles. I just want to know what's going on.'

'What makes you think I might be seeing someone else?'

'The way you've been so distant. When you were making love just now, what were you thinking?' She had turned to look at him; the body of a stranger. Those umber discs – the areolae which he had dreamed of seeing when she stood mending her bicycle. The dark, tangled triangle, and all those doubts, and the inability to find words. The light from the window was behind her; shining through the edge of her hair. He didn't want this. He didn't want to know what she had done, or why. If she had deceived him, then how could he expect her to do anything other than lie when he asked?

King got up from the bed. 'We really don't know each other, do we Jenny?'

Still she stood against the bright window. 'I don't think I could ever get to know you truly, Charles. I don't think you'd let me. I feel sorry for you.'

'Sorry?' he said.

'You've got so many good things about you, and people

who love you. And yet the only thing you can do is hurt them all.'

'Why do you say that?'

'Because you're hurting me. And I love you.'

King began to put on his clothes. He felt somehow ashamed of his nakedness. 'I don't want to hurt you, Jenny. I don't want us to get too close, that's all.'

'Why? What's wrong with being close?' she came and held him – stared hard into his face. 'What's wrong with letting yourself feel something, Charles?'

He moved free of her. 'I do have feelings Jenny, for you. But I don't think it can work.'

'Why? What's gone wrong?'

He was searching for words. 'It was wrong from the start. I wish now . . . I think it would have been better to know you first, as a friend. It all happened too quickly.' She was bewildered by this. 'Jenny, I like you so much, really. But I don't know you. I don't know if I can trust you.'

She held him again. 'It takes time, Charles. I agree, maybe we got off to the wrong start – but that doesn't mean we can't ever make it work. I want to try. I want to make the effort – if only you'll let me through this shell you put around yourself.'

He carried on dressing, and now Jenny began to put on her clothes.

'I wish you'd talk to me, Charles. Whatever it is, you know if you need me . . .'

He wanted to ask her now about why she had been looking through his papers. He felt willing to forgive her anything. He put his arm around her neck, drew her towards himself and kissed her gently.

'If there's somebody else, Charles . . . You would tell me, wouldn't you?'

He said that of course he would.

They had some lunch, and then for further distraction went out for a walk – Kensington Gardens. The weather was brighter now. Couples walking arm in arm, mothers with small children, old people in raincoats. If Jenny had been searching through his belongings, then it could only have been out of this desire to understand him better. It wasn't such a crime. She loved him, and he – he realized it now – he loved her also. When the time was right, he'd ask her about everything, and then it could all be put aside. King held Jenny close to his side. She was telling him stories from her childhood.

They made their way back to her place. Before they reached the entrance to the flats, Jenny said she remembered there were a few things she needed to buy. Charles offered to come to the shop with her, but she said not to bother – she brought out her keys and told him to go and let himself in. She'd try not to be too long; twenty minutes maybe.

He carried on to the front entrance, then up the stairs to her flat. Going into the empty bedsit, he could still smell their sex. It gave him a good feeling.

While going up the stairs, he had resolved that the best way to deal with a situation he found difficult to discuss was to settle things evenly. She had gone through his belongings; he now had every right to reciprocate. In the flat, he began looking in her drawers. There was the underwear with which he was so familiar. He ran his hand through the pile, and felt the soft cloth against his skin. A packet of sanitary towels wedged near the front of the drawer. He lifted out one or two pieces of underwear; ran them against his cheek, and caught their freshly laundered fragrance. Then he pulled open the drawer below. Papers and letters. If she could explore his own life in this way, then why should he not do the same? Photographs, and many letters in the same hand – looking at the sender's address, he saw that they were from the man to whom she had been engaged. There was a vast tract of her life which was completely foreign territory to him. This was what Robert had played on; the fact that you can never know everything about another person; there has to be something you leave to trust. Now a large brown envelope, not stuck down. He pulled out the contents. A photograph of himself – where had she got it from? And a copy of his paper. And a copy of Flood.

He stared at them. Sat down on the edge of the bed, staring at what he had pulled out of the envelope. Drew it all right out. It was a carbon copy of the paper – from when she typed it. And a copy of Flood, just like the two that were in his drawer. This must have been a third.

Never in his life had it felt so devastating to be right. She had searched his drawers – this he could forgive. And taking his photograph, he could understand and forgive. But why did she have these documents, which had allowed Mays to condemn both Robert and himself? Waves of bitterness and recrimination rose to Charles's mouth. He felt his eyes sting with tears.

He stood up. He had to think very quickly; she would soon be back. Not the playhouse of a child, this room; not now. More like a cell – he felt trapped and frightened. Monstrous visions – it was all a great trap; even their initial meeting. Planted there in the street to try and catch out an unsuspecting scientist emerging from the Academy nearby. There had been a policeman around. Why hadn't he helped Jenny with her bike? Monstrous visions.

Thank God he hadn't yet told her anything about Robert. But what should he do now? Pacing up and down with the envelope and its contents. He mustn't let her know he'd found out. No question now of mentioning anything about it – what lies would she come up with? And she would warn Mays. Why had she done it? He thought of her standing against the window, her naked body against the light. He felt an unbearable sorrow – longing for her, betrayed by her. It was all lies – all that stuff about trust. She had only been trying to win his confidence so she could spy on him. A promotion at work, perhaps, or a better flat.

He had her keys – his own spare was still on the key-ring. He removed it. And he put the brown envelope with its contents back where he had found it; checking to make sure there was no evidence of his intrusion. And then he gathered up his things, and went out, leaving the door unlocked behind him. He felt heavy with treachery and loathing.

Going down the flights of stairs, he heard somebody enter at the bottom – it could be her. There was a bend in the landing leading to the door of one of the flats; he hid himself there. Then he heard her footsteps rising – and he watched her back as she carried on up the stairs above him, a bag of groceries in her hand. He longed to call out to her.

When she was out of sight, he went swiftly, quietly down, and out into the street. He felt like a wretched, weeping coward.

On the train going back to Cambridge, he decided what he would have to do. Useless to try and make excuses, or seek explanations. He had to break with Jenny completely – without giving any hint of the reason. Already in his head he had composed the note which he wrote and posted after his arrival home.

I'm sorry, Jenny – I lied to you. You were right; there is someone else. Please don't make it harder by trying to contact me. Thanks for the good times. Charles.

He was surprised, but glad, when he heard nothing from her. He thought she might try to ring. On Monday, King decided that it was time to begin the cycle once more. He invited Joanna out for dinner, and that night they had sex on the floor of his flat. It consoled him to think that the note he had sent was now at least true.

Next day, there was a phone call at last from Robert – it had been more than a week. His voice was hardly less agitated than before – could he come and see Charles that night? He was going to go away to start work on the book. So he had got it after all, Charles thought. Might this mean an end to all their troubles?

Jenny shed many tears for Charles. She would never understand why he had fled so cruelly, but she remained strong in her resolution not to contact him. The letters she wrote to him were all destroyed by her, unsent. It was just as well she had no phone. In time, she would get over him

– in just the same way as she was getting over the one to whom she had been engaged. What she was left with were some souvenirs in a drawer; things she had taken in secret, for fear of asking Charles and seeming too intrusive. The carbon of the paper she typed – so impressive looking. And the things she had found when she dared to pry, on that Friday evening when Charles still had not come home. A photograph he'd never miss, and a spare copy of a pamphlet of essays and poems. Such beautiful things he'd written – must have been him. It was the time when she found that card; *Missing your body. Anne.* Like an ill omen, which had somehow poisoned everything. Anne; she must be something to do with it. Such a clever man, with so many good things about him. Yet such a capacity to hurt those who loved him.

Some time after Robert's call, Charles's phone went again.

'Mays here. When you see your friend tonight. You know.'

24

That evening, Charles King and Robert Waters met for the last time. Mays' phone call alarmed King – his first thought was that Robert must have informed them about his visit. But why should he do that, when it was Robert who was supposed now to be the subject of the enquiry; the one upon whom King had been ordered to spy? Clearly, their moves were being followed.

At around eight o'clock, Robert arrived. He looked pale and serious when Charles opened the door to him; Robert's expression betrayed a fleeting glimpse of inner pain – but then his face immediately changed as he forced a smile, and followed King inside.

'So you got the book, then?'

'Yes, Charles. I wanted to see you before I go.'

King offered Robert a seat, and brought out the bottle of cognac they had opened together a little over a fortnight earlier.

'I'm driving up to Scotland tomorrow. I need a month or two on my own to sort out some material and think about things. Professor Carmichael is letting me use his holiday house.'

Carmichael was the Party representative on the Faculty. It seemed to King that while Mays had such contempt for Robert, there were now others who held him in higher regard.

'I'm glad you got the book, Robert. Congratulations.'

'I'm sorry I've been so paranoid about it.' Robert still seemed agitated. He took off his jacket and laid it on the arm of his chair. 'How's Jenny?'

Charles sipped from his glass. 'Jenny? I've stopped seeing her.'

'Ah. That's too bad. She was a nice girl.'

Robert had his book now. That's what all of this had

been for; all the lies and suffering. So that Robert could go to Scotland and work on a damned book.

'Have you been to see Mays again?'

'Mays? No.' Robert's mask of calm had been disturbed.

'He told me he interviewed you twice.'

Impossible for Robert to hide his anxiety. He eyed King nervously, as if trying to convey some hidden thought to him; or a gesture to make him be quiet.

'I think you're mistaken.'

Then Robert reached into the pocket of his jacket, and brought out a pen and an old bus ticket. Charles watched, bemused, while he scribbled on it, then passed it to him. *Be very careful.*

'How about some more brandy, Charles?'

King poured, then stood up. The two men looked at each other in silence. There was some meaning to all of this, which still was not apparent. Looking at Robert's face, King now saw the eyes of a terrified rabbit. Impossible for them to speak freely.

'It's good that you're going away, Robert. A break for you, I mean. Always best to be on your own when you need to work.'

'Yes, that's what I think. If I stayed here . . . it would all be too difficult. To get things done. So many other demands on one's attention. How's your research going?'

Already they were talking as if in some kind of code. Robert had no interest in Charles's research. Perhaps he was asking if King had been able to find out any more about the police enquiry. He said he was making good progress. 'How long will you be in Scotland?'

'Hard to say. As long as it takes. I've got all the basic facts now – I know what's going on, so to speak. It's a case of making sense of everything.'

Robert now had all the facts; he knew everything. And he knew it was best for him to be apart from Charles. Perhaps he knew that Charles had been ordered to watch him.

'You know, Robert, I've never understood how

historians do "research". In science everything is rather more clear cut. Well-defined problems, and precise methods of investigation.'

'But history is about people's lives Charles – you know I've always said that. It's about investigating people's lives. And there are lots of ways of doing that. When we study history, we're really talking about ourselves. Why it is that we happen to be in a particular place, taking a certain course of action.'

'When often it isn't what we really want to do.'

'That's right, Charles. But there are forces – you always spoke of forces, didn't you? Love, and fear.'

'And the will to survive.'

'That most of all. In the end it's always the will to survive that's strongest.'

'How true, Robert. That's why history is so full of conflict; trust betrayed, loyalties abused. When you're faced with a power far greater than yourself – what choice is there?'

'Like for instance a person who is ordered to do something he finds totally abhorrent – something which will bring pain and suffering, and yet if he disobeys there will be even greater suffering.' There was some further meaning to Robert's words. Already, Charles thought he could see tears in the other man's eyes. Was he giving his permission for Charles to betray him? Or had he himself already committed some abhorrent act? How, after all, had he come to win the contract for the book?

Charles gazed down at his friend – his lost friend. His turn now to speak. 'Yes, the will to survive. Two nations, for example – loyal allies. Each willing to take up arms to help the other. But then a third power arises; a nation whose leaders are driven only by blind ignorance and hatred. And this third power decides to wage a war – just for the sheer hell of it. Simply to inflict its sorrow wherever it sees happiness. What happens to our two peace-loving nations then? They unite, they resist. They swear their alliance will never be broken.'

'But then this third power proves stronger, Charles. It makes the shrewdest tactical move. Its forces occupy the land in the middle; the borderland between its two opponents. Cuts them off from each other – makes communication so dangerous as to be impossible.'

'That's right, Robert. That would be the shrewdest thing. And then it can fight each one separately; lay siege. Gradually spread fear and intimidation – so that soon our two nations are full of doubt and mistrust. And once the invader has bled them dry of hope, he can make the final strike. To each side, he gives the ultimatum: help me, or die.'

'Yes, Charles – it's the best tactic; make life impossible for both sides. And then leave them with that terrible choice: to join forces with the oppressor, or else perish. And it's not a simple choice; not a matter of making some heroic sacrifice. Because this is a nation of people – women and children. Innocent people. But still there's some resistance – an attempt to help the other suffering nation. So the oppressor relents a little. He says that he will be lenient; if forces are joined, then the other side need only be taught a lesson – only limited action.'

Charles understood everything now. He could see at what cost Robert had been given his precious book. 'It would be a terrible dilemma, wouldn't it?' Charles said. 'To have to betray a friend – but only a little. To teach him a lesson. So as to save both. And to save all those innocent people.'

'Mostly to save the innocents, Charles. It's the women and children who are the most important element in history – because they're always the first victims.'

Anne and Duncan. What would Robert not do to protect them? Charles moved towards the piano. He ran his finger along the top – it needed dusting. Jenny did it little more than a week earlier.

'Thanks for the history lesson, Robert. I'm sure your book will be very good.'

'The book means nothing to me, Charles. It's only words on paper.'

Charles sat down at the piano. 'A shame you didn't bring your violin, Robert. Remember how we used to play together?'

'We should have practised more. We never did manage to get the Kreutzer right, did we?'

'We never got anything right.' He turned to look at the other man; the nervous, helpless creature. Mays had won.

Robert got up, and then went to the bathroom. His jacket still lay across the arm of the chair from which he had risen.

He had been ordered to spy on King – it was all clear now. The simplest tool of persecution; to set people one against the other – to spread fear and suspicion. What crime had Charles committed? It would only be a fine, or perhaps six months. Mays could not have recruited Robert – it must be the Party who had enlisted him. The vetting would have been handled by Section Five; they had persuaded Robert to watch Charles, just as the police wanted Charles to keep an eye on Robert. A battle of two Government departments. But if each one of them, Charles and Robert, played his part well enough, then what was there for either to fear?

As long as Robert handled his side of it properly. He was trying to warn King; was that not sufficient proof of his good faith? And yet Charles knew that for Robert things were not so simple. There was Anne, and Duncan. Was his warning to Charles not also a plea for forgiveness?

Charles lifted Robert's jacket, and ran his hand into the inside pocket. An address book. Only a name, to keep Mays off his back. He might need Mays if Section Five made problems. A name, any name for starters. It would be somewhere inconspicuous – not amongst the addresses of family and colleagues. Yes – here. A loose slip of paper inside the back cover. John: 376812. It had to be. He said it three times until he remembered the number. Everything put back. He returned to his place.

Robert came in. He picked up his jacket – paused as he lifted it from the arm of the chair. He put it on, then looked up to meet King's eyes. Thinking about it long afterwards, King would remember what he saw now as the worn face of a man already dead.

'What time do you leave tomorrow?'

'First thing. It's a long drive. I want to make an early start.'

'Drive safely.'

'I will. And look after yourself, Charles. Always remember to look after yourself.' There was nothing more to say.

'Give my love to Anne and Duncan.'

'Of course.' Robert paused. 'Charles . . . if anything were to happen to me. I don't want to be morbid – but I'm not used to going away and leaving them. It's a long drive. If anything happened . . . you'd take care of them, wouldn't you?'

'You know what they both mean to me.'

'Yes. I've always known that. Goodbye Charles.'

'Good luck. With the book.'

Robert reached out his hand – Charles grasped it firmly. It seemed as if there was something more that Robert needed to say; as if he were struggling to find words. But none came. Their hands remained locked in a gesture whose full meaning each could only guess at. Finally, they embraced.

'Goodbye Charles.'

And then he left. It was the last time they would see each other.

Next day, King got a phone call at work. It was Mays again, wanting him to come to the police station. Charles already knew what he would say, before he was shown into the interview room.

'I don't spy on my friends, Inspector Mays. There's no reason why I should. If you want to arrest me then go ahead, though I don't know what you'll charge me with. Otherwise, you can go to hell.'

Mays remained calm. 'You're a subversive. You write horrible seditious pamphlets. You consort with perverts. I can arrest you for anything I like, and I can have you put away for as long as I like. Are you going to help me?'

'Go to hell.'

Mays opened the drawer of his desk and brought out a large brown envelope. 'Waters has gone to Scotland. While he's away I want you to go to his house – visit his wife. And when you get the chance, I want you to leave this hidden somewhere among his papers. Just give us a ring when it's done.'

He threw the envelope across the desk onto King's lap. Lifting open the flap to examine the contents, King saw a dog-eared foreign magazine. The cover showed a naked man.

'It's not a lot to ask, Dr. King. I could easily have had Waters tailed, or turned his house upside down looking for something that would incriminate him, but it really isn't necessary. This way, it's a lot less painful for everyone concerned. I know you're both guilty. Proof is nothing more than a formality, for the sake of the paperwork. Just do this little thing for me, and I'll forget all about your dubious past. The slate will be wiped clean. You've got three days. Let me know when it's done.'

King went back out into the daylight. He had already made his decision. There would be no more betrayals – what could they do to him? Six months at worst. The time had come for him to call a halt to this spiral of madness. He put the envelope and its contents into the first litter bin he passed. For the first time in two weeks, he felt happy.

When he went back to work, he found Joanna alone, typing. He whispered in her ear, and asked if she'd like to come to his place that night. She gave a nod without saying anything; her fingers still clattering on the keys of the typewriter.

King would do nothing. That was his great decision. Mays could go to hell. Had they perhaps threatened Jenny like that, as well? Made her search through Charles's things? But then again – why? There was still something missing; something which Charles didn't understand, but maybe Robert did. He had all the facts now.

Later, Joanna came to his flat. They had sex once more on the carpet where they had first lain two nights previously. So unlike Jenny – so business-like. When they finished, she got up and walked briskly to the bathroom. Even when she was naked she had the same way of moving; the same haughty air. She came back with a toilet roll, which she handed to King, who was still lying exhausted on the floor.

King was not usually given to opening up his heart to a woman after he had sex with her; he did not regard the intimacy of physical intercourse as an excuse for unburdening his soul. But on this occasion, he wanted to talk. He felt proud of the stand he had made against Mays – he had told him to go to hell.

Joanna was wiping her crotch with toilet paper – an action as smoothly honed as when she cleaned her typewriter. Her figure was towering over him as he lay on the carpet – her perfect figure. Her face was not pretty; she had an arrogant look. But her body was one of the most perfect that Charles had ever seen; finely proportioned, and with the lean athleticism of a greyhound.

King wanted to tell her everything. He wanted to tell her about Robert, and Mays. He even wanted to tell her about Jenny. He said nothing. Now Joanna was moving about the room, stretching like a ballerina. Her perfect body. She gave a little yawn. Then she came and sat across him; straddling his groin.

He was thinking about Jenny, and how he must have hurt her.

She repositioned herself slightly, and fell to playing with his genitals; reaching to push his dormant flesh from one side to the other. Lifting and stretching the pink stub of his penis, like a toy.

'I once knew a man who could come twice. Like a multiple orgasm. Have you ever been able to do that?'

He told her no, and she said perhaps she shouldn't be talking about other men. He told her he didn't mind – but this only made her say more on the subject.

'And there was one who made me give him a blow-job

192

every morning. He was an architect. He'd push my head down onto him.'

'Why did you put up with him?'

She shrugged. 'He was convenient, at the time.'

Charles thought about Jenny, and that tiny bedsit. The vase of flowers, and the photographs on the wall, of her family. The letters she had kept in her drawer. He had loved her simplicity – her weakness. And it was her weakness that had made her betray him; he still didn't understand how, or why – perhaps Robert knew the whole story by now. But it was precisely what was so good about her that had led things to go so terribly wrong.

Joanna was still playing with him. She had made him go hard. She held the shaft aloft like a flag. Then laid it down. She stood up, and began to dress.

25

Three days went past and Charles made no effort to contact Anne. The following week, he went home as usual at lunchtime to play the piano. Still he felt exhilarated by his defiance – and he had heard nothing more from Mays. Sitting himself at the keyboard, he chose the score of the Diabelli Variations. He was soon engrossed in the music.

To see why King should have selected that piece to play, let us first recall the strange origin of the work. In 1819, the publisher Anton Diabelli sent a little waltz theme he had written to fifty or so of the leading composers in Vienna. He wanted each to write a variation, which he would publish as a sort of compendium of contemporary musical taste. Beethoven (who was already working on the Ninth Symphony and the Missa Solemnis) dismissed the waltz as a 'cobbler's patch' – nothing more than vamping, and unworthy of his attention. Even so, the theme began to suggest to him some latent possibility (strange, how the most persistent ideas are often the most irritatingly trivial). During the next four years, Beethoven produced no less than thirty-three variations on Diabelli's little waltz. He alone would give Diabelli his compendium of musical taste; there was a fughetta in the style of Bach, a study after the manner of Cramer – even a quotation from Mozart's *Don Giovanni*. Characteristically of Beethoven, it was an act of defiance – and a joke.

When King sat down at the keyboard, he still felt thrilled by his own act of defiance against Mays. Flood had been nothing more than a feeble prank – a cobbler's patch. And now it was over – King had called 'enough'. Robert could write his book, and they could forget all about it.

When the telephone rang, Charles ignored it.

The Diabelli Variations, in addition to being Beethoven's greatest piano composition, is also one of his most difficult. A full sixty minutes in performance, and a piece which requires a considerable technique. It was one of the most demanding pieces which King could possibly select. An act of defiance, and of celebration. It was the punchline of a joke at Mays' expense.

But then the flow of sound interrupted. The doorbell. King swore, went and answered, and saw two policemen who showed a warrant, entered, and began to search his flat. One took the sitting room, the other the bedroom; opening drawers, checking shelves.

'I told you, we've got a warrant to search the premises.'

'But why?'

'Because we suspect you might be in possession of illegal substances.'

'What? Do you mean drugs?'

The score remained open on the piano where King had stopped. It seemed that the joke still was not over. He stood and watched in disbelief while the two policemen quickly went about their work. One of them was checking the entrance passage which led off to the bathroom and bedroom. He lifted a corner of the carpet, near the bathroom door, and called out to his colleague. 'Got it.' He was picking up a small polythene pouch with something dark inside.

King protested: 'For Christ's sake, you've just planted that.'

They took him to the police station. In the interview room, Mays ordered him to sit down.

'You stupid bastard, King.'

'You had them plant it in my flat – anyone can see that.'

'You're no use to any of us here now. It's like this; we can charge you, you'll get six months, and you'll be sacked from your job. Or else you can make things easier for yourself; resign now, we drop charges, and you'll be rehabilitated.'

'What do you mean?'

'Somebody thinks you need to be taught a lesson. And I don't fucking blame them. They'll give you another job somewhere out of harm's way where you can learn to behave yourself. Don't think you've got any choice in the matter; you either do it now, or else in six months' time when you come out of prison.'

When he returned home, the score still lay open where he had left it. It had been a premature celebration. Strange, how the most trivial thing can grow, become transformed, and have consequences of the most grave and colossal kind. He had written an article in defence of the rights of homosexuals; he had included a true but seditious statement concerning a former Minister for Home Affairs. And so the pamphlet had been retained in a file for five years, lying dormant, until it could be brought out and his life could be totally changed. Strange how a harmless trifle can be the origin of a process of transformation – of variation – which is far beyond anything it might seem to merit. King sat on the piano stool and looked at the printed notes without laying his hands on the keys. Mays had indeed won – his threat had not proved idle. And such a blatant manner in which the threat had been realized! Was it even necessary for those two constables to go through the charade of searching for something they had already brought with them?

Now King was to be 'rehabilitated'; they were going to try and transform him – strip him of his pride and will; lay him low, so that he would emerge humbled and obedient.

He turned the pages of the Diabelli Variations. Gazed at that final chord – the final punchline. A chord which is resolved harmonically, and yet leaves something unanswered; an inversion of the tonic chord, which misses the beat. A punchline which can leave you laughing, or else puzzled and bewildered.

The following day he received a letter offering him a post teaching maths in a school in Leeds. He was being taught a lesson. He went to see Anne.

'Robert knew this would happen,' he told her, 'I'm sure of it. What's going on?'

She said she knew nothing. She was cold and unwilling to talk to him. Duncan came running in to show Charles a

196

toy train which his father had given him before leaving. Anne drew the boy to her side, and stared at King.

'You'd better go.'

Later, he handed in his resignation – so smooth and easy, the whole process. In a land where every step involved a mountain of forms in triplicate, this move was to be the easiest he had ever made. He was allocated a flat in Leeds, not far from the school where he would work. Vague references were made to its additional proximity to the university. After a few years of penance they might give him a job in the physics department there.

He had a month's notice. Joanna said she was sorry he had decided to leave; King explained to her that he had no choice in the matter. She seemed alarmed, but didn't try to find out any more about it. During the remaining four weeks before the move, their affair continued fitfully. Charles told her he would try and return to Cambridge at weekends to do research.

Shortly before his month ran out, Charles learned the news that Robert had been killed in a car accident. They had taught Robert an even harder lesson, Charles thought. He had begun to drive home from Scotland; it was night, raining. The car must have gone too fast into a bend; it left the road and went through the barrier, then down into a ravine. He had died instantly.

Charles went to see Anne again. She seemed less hostile now that she needed him. They sat together in silence. When Duncan came in and asked again when Daddy would be coming home, she said simply 'not yet.'

King had not forgotten his promise to Robert, but his attempts to offer help all met with swift rebuttal. She would need to think things through, but they would probably move away from Cambridge. They were going to stay with her sister in York for a while.

Then she went and fetched a sealed letter addressed to Charles. Robert had written to her from Scotland, enclosing this additional message for King, which was to be given to him 'if anything happened'.

'He knew they might try and kill him, Charles. I don't know what it was you got him involved in, and I don't think I want to know – at least not yet. But I do want to say that I forgive you. I know he was your friend, and you would never have done anything to hurt him. He thought the world of you, Charles.'

He took the letter from her, and she did not resist when he took hold of her hand, and lightly stroked it. There were many things he would have liked to ask her.

'Anne, I want to help you in whatever way I can. You know that to me, Duncan is almost like my own son.'

She flinched. 'He's Robert's son. He is now, and he always will be.'

Charles regretted his words. But there would be time to make amends – long years in which to try and earn forgiveness.

When he went home, he opened Robert's letter. Difficult at first to make sense of the crabbed writing – and almost as if starting in mid-sentence; the erratic script in blue ink. Letters indistinct and corrected, scored out and rewritten; hasty, urgent writing – a valediction, and a confession, and gradually the forming of a pattern, gradually everything becoming clear. After reading it twice, Charles thought of destroying it. But he decided that this would be the greatest crime of all.

It was the final chord – the final resolution. And it was a great, terrible joke which did not leave him laughing. First, he considered writing a letter to Jenny, apologizing to her for having believed that she had betrayed him. But he had never told her why he had left her so cruelly, and he could see no hope of reconciliation. His affair with Joanna – that arrogant woman with her perfect body – was a kind of purging, a wiping clean – an attempt to erase, or else to justify his sins against Jenny. He would never try to contact her. He felt he owed her this final act of kindness.

He sat himself at the piano. It was not Beethoven he chose, but Bach. There would be time yet for him to weep for Robert, and for Jenny – but now he needed to be reminded that there was still some sanity in the world. He chose the Goldberg Variations.

A work very different in character from Beethoven's set – but another grand piece in variation form; thirty variations on a slow, gentle aria. A work of symmetry and balance. There would be time yet to regret everything, and then at last to regret no more.

Let us recall the strange story which Spitta has told, concerning the origin of Bach's great composition. There was a nobleman called Keyserling, who was troubled by insomnia. During sleepless nights, he would ask his young harpsichordist Goldberg to sit in the next room playing soothing music. Keyserling commissioned Bach to produce a piece for Goldberg to play – and the result was that huge set (even longer than Beethoven's). Pure, disciplined, abstract music.

Beethoven took his theme as the basis for a process of transformation – so that the final conclusion is unimaginably distant from the beginning. But in Bach, the theme is never lost – its bass line is present, unaltered, throughout the whole of the thirty variations, until at last the theme returns, and the music ends. The journey has been a miraculous process of standing still. Music for an insomniac aristocrat. Does it matter, that Spitta's famous story is almost certainly false? And if we could discover with certainty who was the true author of the gentle aria which is the basis of those variations, then how might this affect our attitude to the music which Bach wrote?

Pure, disciplined, abstract music. There would be time yet to reflect on Robert's words – his last words. And perhaps Anne would one day allow King to make amends, somehow.

He heard about the inquest, and the verdict satisfied him – an accident. Why subject Anne to further suffering? And then he went to Leeds, and became a schoolteacher – at first he loathed the job, but after a while he came to feel a strange sense of release. Although he returned to Cambridge most weekends, the research he tried to continue came to interest him less and less. Something was changing inside him; the children he taught were helping him to rediscover the child within himself. Life was easier now. He felt more free than he had ever done.

He looks older now – how can twenty years go by without leaving their trace? But they have treated him kindly – he still has something of his younger looks. He comes home from the university, and finds Duncan in the front room, that awkward young man, sitting on the floor with his back to the sofa, reading a book of stories by Alfredo Galli.

Charles says hello, and receives a grunt in response. He goes to the tiny spare room he calls his study, puts his briefcase on the desk, then goes back to the sitting room. Duncan has moved now; gone to his bedroom and closed the door. And although Duncan has undergone far greater physical alteration in the intervening years, there is still something in him of that four year old child with a toy train, asking when his father would return. King's 'rehabilitation' served only to liberate him once and for all – Duncan's sentence, on the other hand, has been much harder. Perhaps his moodiness is simply his mother's inheritance. But Charles can see how every part of Duncan's life has grown beneath the shade of unexplained tragedy. Couldn't even stick it at university – when he left his mother in York and moved to Leeds. History, like Robert. But he couldn't stick it. Anne didn't want him to stay with Charles and Joanna, but it was the simplest solution – the most practical. And Charles was doing it for Duncan, not for Anne. He was doing it for Robert.

It's April – a fine early evening in Spring. Already, a year has elapsed since that *annus mirabilis*, when the old order finally gave way and collapsed. Those protest marches; the students, and the workers, and the ordinary people going forward together. Now the talk is of democracy, freedom and rebuilding.

When Duncan reappears from his bedroom, King asks if his mother will be visiting him again at the weekend – but

Duncan says no, not this weekend, since he'll be going to London. He intends to go to the Office of Public Records.

'What do you want to go there for? You don't think they'll have a file on you?'

'I want to find out what happened to Dad.'

Charles asks him where he'll stay, whether he can afford the fare – and does it have to be this weekend? Duncan says it can't wait – already there's talk of closing the files again, because of all the trouble it's causing. And Charles says it might be for the best if they were closed quickly – since the past is better left alone.

'What do you mean by that?'

'What I mean is that under the Communists we were all guilty, all of us. Everyone's got something to hide. I did things that I'm not proud of now – and I'm sure your father was the same.'

'Oh you're sure are you? And who the hell do you think you are to tell me about my father?'

'I knew him, Duncan. He was a good man. And he had his weaknesses – just like you and me.'

No point in arguing about it. Charles always knew that Duncan would have to learn the truth one day.

The sound of a key in the front door – Joanna. She calls out as she enters. 'It's me, darling,' then comes in and presents her cheek for Charles to kiss. 'Duncan, I told you I'd wash that tee-shirt if you'd leave it in the basket. Look at it – it's appalling. Aaah, Smiley . . .' the cat has appeared from somewhere, and struts towards her with its tail held stiffly in the air. 'How is mummy's lickle baby . . .?' she bends down to tickle its chin. 'Run off my feet at the surgery today, Charlie. And they didn't have any chicken left – it's lamb for supper.'

Duncan would have to find out eventually. Charles watches him go sulking back to his bedroom, while Joanna goes to the kitchen and begins to put things in the fridge. He sits down at the piano – it occurs to him to play something, but he can't decide which piece.

Joanna calls to him from the kitchen. 'I was watching

the starlings on the way home. Have you ever noticed how they swirl around – it's beautiful. Made me wish I had a camera with me. Though I don't suppose it would come out.' Sounds of cupboard doors being opened and closed, and the rustle of polythene, and Joanna calling out to him. 'How is it that they can all fly together like that? They all decide at the same time to go one way or the other. Makes you wonder if they've got some kind of telepathy.'

Charles can't decide what to play. 'Yes, I've thought about that too, Joanna. I thought about it for years. In the end, I concluded that they're simply following the air currents.'

'Oh Charlie, you scientists are so unromantic.'

The scores of Beethoven and Bach lie beside him on the floor. He struggles now, to come to a decision. Would it be kinder of us to tell him that it makes no difference which choice he makes?

PART FIVE

26

How easy it is, in fiction, to sweep aside two decades. The merest touch of the pen, and we see faces growing older, hair turning from black to grey. The better part of a lifetime can disappear in a literary ellipsis.

It's nearly two years now since Eleonora left me. An insignificant lump, that was how it started. Strange, how the most trivial, unimportant looking things can go on to have such profound consequences. Perhaps if I hadn't allowed her to pretend early on that it really couldn't be anything to worry about. But why go through all that again?

Nearly two years since she left me, that's all. How long it seems, since I saw her alive and healthy! And yet that day when we first met, twenty years ago, feels like yesterday – whatever it means for a memory to seem 'like yesterday'. Difficult to say with any certainty what the sensation of remembering actually is. I know how to judge that a tree is thirty yards away, or that a stone weighs a pound or two. But how to reach the conclusion that a past event feels as if it occurred a year ago? Or twenty?

I met her on a train, not unlike the one on which I am now sitting. She was intrigued by my foreign accent – she asked me how it was that a physicist from Britain had come to be teaching English in Italy. And I told her the circumstances which had brought me here.

A colleague had sent me an invitation to a conference in Milan. It would, I knew, be a rather tedious meeting – I had already lost interest in research by then. I had finally realized that I would never be able to live up to the expectations my late father had of me. I only went because I wanted to see Italy. I remember arriving at Milan railway station, harassed and sweating in my grey suit. I had left one circus, and arrived in another. My colleague put me up for a while. I skipped the conference, outstayed my visa, and then applied for political asylum.

I had to persuade them that I was being persecuted in some way. In fact, it was not persecution from which I sought refuge, but rather from politics itself. I had come from a country where every word, deed, gesture had its place in a vast ideological vocabulary. I wanted to be able to live without constant reference to the state, that was all. The regime I had left was, it is now clear, really rather more benign than most. The English have a passion for moderation in everything – even totalitarianism. The whole thing, now that it has gone, can be seen to have been comically genteel.

I sought asylum – I have to confess it – because I liked the look of the place. It was sunny, the food was good, and the women well dressed. Easy at the time to couch my aspirations in the language of political oppression. Really, I was a refugee from drabness. From tinned peas, and rain.

We met on the train. I offered to give her lessons in English, and during my second visit to her flat in Milan, we found ourselves together on that Turkish rug. Only two English lessons – two pretended lessons.

The question of love was of no importance then or subsequently. We desired each other – in a sense which was almost abstract. And I knew at once that I would marry this woman. At the time, I didn't even think I liked her, and yet there seemed to be an awesome inevitability about the idea of us coming together.

Yes, inevitability was how I must have thought of it at the time; I regarded Eleonora as something which had been somehow preordained. Or at any rate, I had the feeling that the time had come for me to choose the partner with whom I should share my life (I was in my early thirties) – and it was Eleonora who came and sat opposite me on the train.

Of course, nothing in life is inevitable, other than its eventual end. It was chance which had brought me to Italy, and chance which had placed Eleonora in my compartment. In those days, I still felt some residual need to argue that somehow things had all been arranged for me by some unseen power – that everything was 'for the best'. The idea of historical inevitability is little more than this; an excuse for events rather than an explanation.

There are many who say that the mad regime in Britain from which I had escaped was itself inevitable – the experience of the thirties and the war years being irrefutable proof. The alternatives seem impossible only because they didn't happen. It's left to writers now to dream of all the other equally probable outcomes which history could have chosen – like that genre of novel now appearing, based on the premise that the German occupation never occurred, and that the Communists were not elected in 1947 (though even if the Germans had never invaded, the Communists would probably have been elected anyway). Such fantasies are amusing enough, with their outlandish scenarios in which monarchy and aristocracy still exist – an excuse to write fulsome descriptions of garden parties, balls and society events of a kind which lasted well into this century. And perhaps they are really not so outlandish after all – already, I hear, they are bringing back the debutantes' 'coming out' ball. Where have these people been hiding for the last forty years?

The speculations of the 'alternative history' writers are simply a corollary to the 'Gallian' philosphy which I espouse so wholeheartedly. The historical events with which fate has chosen to entertain and torture us are little more than numbers on the throw of a die.

And it was Eleonora who came and sat opposite me. She became my student, my lover, and then my wife. Had I missed that train (in other words, if I had been quick enough to catch the earlier one which I was aiming for) then Eleonora would never have happened – who knows where I would now be, what I would now be doing? Not writing this, I'm certain. What, I wonder, would my father have made of the meandering course which my life has taken – so unlike the confident torrent of achievement with which he preceded me?

Why do I mention my father again? Because I broke off

from writing to go to the toilet, and as I pulled up the zipper ... but I think I told you that story a while ago. You will have noticed by now, that I have an unendearing habit of repeating myself. It used to irritate my father considerably – he would stop me in mid-flow: 'Yes, you've told me already.' And I would fall silent.

When I was young, he would take me out for walks – and I would always be asking him questions. Once I asked him what light was made of, and he said it was made of waves, like the sea. So that I wondered why light didn't make your eye wet. But then I asked him again another time, and he told me he'd heard something about light being made of lots of particles – and so in order to settle the matter, he presented me a few days later with a book about physics, which told me that light was made neither of waves nor of particles, but could be regarded as consisting of either, depending on how you looked at it. Which made physics seem like the sort of subject I would enjoy. And it told me that the speed of light through space would always appear the same to you – no matter how fast you travelled – so that a beam of light is something with which you can never catch up. In my life, my father was like a beam of light. He illuminated so many things for me, and yet they were to remain forever beyond my reach.

It was he who made me learn the piano – I think he dreamed of me becoming a great concert pianist, but I never came up to the standard he would have liked. He would listen to me practise – once I had become quite good. He would wait in silence as the notes flowed out. Then I would play a false one, and I would hear him grunt in dissatisfaction. Years later, I played for Eleonora. I chose an easy piece, and gave it the sort of concentration you'd apply to a cliff face which you were hanging from by your fingernails. And halfway through, I lost my grip for a bar or two. 'That was nice,' she said when I finished. 'Shame about the mistakes.'

I knew from the start that we would be married. I admired her – even on the train, when we first met, I was filled with admiration for her coolness, so elegant and controlled. If I had been born a woman, I would have wanted to be like her.

And I grew to love her – it surprised me, the warmth I came to feel for this chilly creature. Initially I loved her as I might love a piece of music. Later, it was more like the feeling one would have towards a blood relative – a loyalty, and the sense of comfort which comes with familiarity. Now I miss her terribly. An insignificant lump – that was how it started.

But I was talking about my father. Once he knew that I would never be a brilliant pianist, he set his hopes on my ability in maths and science. When I went to university to study physics, it was taken for granted that I would do well, and go on to do a Ph.D. It was only once I had got past even that hurdle, and was beginning to do my own research, that I realized that I had been propelled along a course that I had never really wanted. I was not very good at research – which is all about following the literature, and making academic contacts, and keeping abreast of all the latest developments. I knew now why light is both a wave and a particle – and I didn't really care to know any more than that. My imagination had been filled to the brim with all the ideas I had been packing into it over the years. I didn't want to learn anything more. I tried to tell my father that I was thinking of changing my career, but I could never find the courage to come straight out with it. I knew that unless I could fulfil all his expectations of me, then I would have failed. And so I failed.

I was in my mid-twenties when he died – only beginning to get to know him. Just as well, perhaps, that he didn't live to see how things turned out. Not only in my life, but the state of things generally. He was an ardent socialist – current events would have been such a disappointment to him. It's easy to forget that the system which we all now despise so much was begun by idealists, dreamers – people who believed in freedom from exploitation, and the right to a decent standard of living. How can I wholeheartedly despise a system of which he was such a committed supporter?

He claimed to have been a Communist since the thirties, when he was still in his teens. No one knew then what Stalin was really doing. Easy now to regard them all as naive fools, duped by propaganda. How could we make such a mistake nowdays, now that cable TV shows us the world as it really is?

After his death I carried on in academic research for another five years, unable to make the decision to quit – I could think of nothing else to do. My escape to Italy was as much an escape from his memory as from anything else – I can admit this now. Even in death, his figure haunts me. It was the only way I could free myself from the destiny which had been charted for me – a life of futile struggle and disappointment.

My colleague in Milan said he would try and get me a lecturing job, but I had had enough of it. I found myself a flat in Cremona – cheaper than Milan, and quieter – and I offered private tuition in English. It gave me such a wonderful sense of freedom, teaching something which was as easy and natural to me as breathing. I had had enough of struggling.

I told Eleonora none of this, when I first met her on a train twenty years ago, while I was returning from a short visit to Naples and Pompeii. As far as she was concerned I was a refugee scientist, and hence fascinating. Our affair began during the second English lesson. Then I would take the train every weekend to Milan to be with her – I could have seen her more often, but this was the only time she chose to spare me. During the week, I'm sure she would forget all about me. I suspected she might have another man, and this only added to her appeal. If she were cheating me with someone else, then by the same token, she was cheating him with me – which made me feel quite honoured. My own loyalty, on the other hand, was total. Loyalty not only to her, but to my conviction that what I was doing was 'for the best'.

I was taking the train to see her. It was some weeks after we first met – I was still reading the same book by Alfredo Galli which had stimulated our first conversation. I'm such a slow reader, and so easily distracted – and usually during my weekend journeys I would only inch forward a page or two. I was sitting alone in the compartment, when a girl came and sat opposite me.

The scene reminded me at once of my first encounter with Eleonora – yet this girl was very different. She was small and almost boyish, with short black hair, and eye-lashes which curled and caught the light. I watched her over the top of my book, between reading the same page again and again. Eventually I felt my lack of page turning might be rather obvious, so I noisily flicked forward – by now totally lost with the story I was supposed to be reading.

Eventually we began a conversation, and in the course of our brief journey together, I feel that I came to know her better than I would understand Eleonora even after eighteen years of marriage. And yet I never learned her name! In all our talk, we never bothered to introduce ourselves. She told me about her life, and how she was having a troubled relationship with a boy – and I told her about Eleonora, and my father, and all the other things I have told you here, as well as lots more besides. The little train compartment became like a confessional – I was so glad that no-one came to disturb us! You can spend a life-time trying to communicate with someone you love, but then one day you meet a stranger and for a brief moment you feel the unique experience of your soul connecting with that of another person. We reached our destination, we got off the train, and I never saw her again.

I had no wish to form a liaison with this woman – pretty and charming as she was. I had Eleonora – I was happy with her. And my loyalty was absolute. I already knew, from the way I had betrayed the memory of my father, how bitter the taste of disloyalty could be.

But if I had not had Eleonora, then I would have fallen

in love with that unknown woman there and then. So sweet, and warm – how could I have resisted? If, some weeks earlier, I had caught my intended train, then there would have been no Eleonora. And then I might now be in the arms of that charming girl whose name (how I regret it!) I never even learned, though I knew so much else about her.

But I didn't find it difficult to put her out of my mind. Easy to be callous with one's emotions at the time – only to suffer the consequences later on. What was it, that brought the memory of that girl back into my mind after a gap of ten years?

You see – another decade has slipped away in a single line! Eleonora and I were married. I would come home each evening from my job at the English school in Milan, and I would find her, in our flat in Cremona, sitting with her feet up, immersed in a book. Those awful slippers! They were purple and fluffy. I tried to find sexier ones for her, but soon realized that there is no such thing as a sexy pair of slippers.

We made love one night – I see our bodies, as if from above. I try to visualize it. She asked me what I was thinking. I said 'nothing', and went to the bathroom. What was it, while I was standing naked on the cold floor, that made me think of that other girl I had met long ago? And those two people, meeting on a train. Giovanna, I would call her; and he was Duncan. In my mind I could see her again, sitting opposite me – the mysterious girl whose name I never learned. And yet her face had lain hidden in my memory for ten years! I couldn't even be sure that it was the same face which I now saw – perhaps the memory had undergone some hidden process of alteration during the intervening years.

When I went back to bed, I told my wife nothing of the strange vision I had experienced – and still I said nothing, during the following weeks and months, when the vision returned, again and again – a story now; a novel, which one day I would write, if only I could overcome my guilt in imagining this lost girl while I lay with my wife. How could I be so cruel and heartless as to let my mind stray into such thoughts? Even, years later, as my wife lay – as she lay in hospital. Plumbed with rubber tubes, and grey-faced as stone. An idea sent to torture me – that instead of standing there in despair, I might be happy and contented in the arms of the other woman, surrounded by our many children, with a peaceful old age to look forward to. How can anyone be so mean and selfish as I was then, to think such a thing? If only thoughts were not such untameable creatures.

And now I am alone in the world. Still, each day, I take the train from Cremona to Milan to teach in the English school. And still, even now that Eleonora has left me, I am troubled by thoughts of all those other lives which I abandoned and lost – that great tree of possibilities.

I thought it would all be so easy, once I got the first chapter sorted out – and yet I still can't get it right; that scene on the train. Twice I have tried to bring them together – Duncan and Giovanna – and yet each time I have failed. Perhaps I'm destined to spend the rest of my life rewriting it. The tree of possibilities branches so quickly, that it soon becomes impossible to follow with any degree of completeness, all the many middles and ends which can spring from a single beginning.

But now I shall try once more. It is a story about two people who meet on a train. And it begins with an image; the image of a motor car crashing through a barrier and tumbling down a hill.

27

It sounded no different from pushing an old, empty car down over a hill in order to get rid of it; the speed at which it had approached the bend, and the efforts of the driver to save himself – if he had had time to make any – did nothing to alter the impression that it was only useless junk which was crashing heavily in the darkness through low bushes. And the hillside was being littered with the contents of a suitcase – socks, underwear, trousers – and the contents of a briefcase also, or perhaps a file or folder – papers were being scattered. All of this, they would have to go over carefully afterwards.

Robert Waters spent three weeks in Scotland. It was during his return journey – at the very beginning of that return journey – that his car left the road, and he was killed.

Had you been there to see it, you might have been disappointed by the ordinariness – indeed, the banality of the scene. The white Morris Commonwealth hitting the barrier, the heavy crunching. All quite undramatic – not at all like the films. Not in slow motion, but still ponderous and heavy, and not a good way to die. And all his things coming out of the door when it flew open, when it was pulled back on itself and crumpled under the body of the car then reappeared as the car turned again, the door flapping like an injury and the suitcase opening on impact. The briefcase opening on impact. Or perhaps a file or a folder.

And when you aren't looking out of the window of the train you're reading a story by Alfredo Galli.

A story which begins strangely, obliquely – the sentences emerging from the page as if at an angle. The first paragraphs set the scene; there is a train, passengers on board patiently awaiting the eventual end of their journey – people who are barely described, whose existence is only hinted at. It is left to the reader to imagine them – passengers who are scanning newspapers and magazines, or dealing with their fidgeting children. These details are not explicitly stated (in a short story, one must be ruthless with excess verbal luggage), but it's not unreasonable to assume that they are there – for are they not always? (especially the fidgeting children). Where has this train come from? It has come from the first sentence of the story, chugging out into existence as if from a dark tunnel. Discarded words fall in its wake like cinders; words already read, comprehended and digested – words which continue to propel it along its path. And sentences tumble onto the tracks, then blow away in the slipstream to be lost forever.

Approaching the bend. Night. Not a trap of gravel and misleading roadsigns, but from somewhere in the darkness, perhaps, the dull pop of a gun, and then the white car hitting the barrier, rolling and turning. Crashing down the hillside. And had you been there, Duncan, had you been able to see it as it really was, instead of continually recreating it in your mind – your father's white Morris Commonwealth approaching the bend; coming fast towards the bend. An obstacle, perhaps? He brakes; no loss of speed. Brakes harder – nothing at all, and already too late. The car hitting the barrier.

A story about a train. Some pages go by – elegant similes, arcane vocabulary. The author brings two people together – a man and a woman. They sit opposite one another in silence. The story describes their unease – first from his point of view, then from hers; an unease which is mutual, shared – and yet this thing which they share is what also keeps them apart.

Neither speaks. Can a story really be about two people sitting in silence? Already another page and a half has gone by without a word being uttered. There are observations of the carriage, of the view from the window, of their bodily sensations – but no dialogue. You long for some quotation marks (so good for 'breaking up the flow'); prolonged silences make you uneasy – it doesn't take much effort to say something mundane about the weather or the state of the train. But these two are settling down for a sustained bout of wordlessness. You've had enough of this story for the time being. You close the book and allow yourself to daydream.

The train has already reached the first station. A girl is looking at the empty seat opposite you, and asking if it's free. The sort of girl with whom you might have an interesting conversation – and yet you stay hidden behind the safety of your book. She pulls out a fat paperback and becomes likewise immersed.

And when you reopen the book, you try to read the story again from the start. Once more, the train is pulling out from the opening lines; once more, words flutter and fall behind it as it speeds along the tracks. You follow again from the beginning; the two people sitting opposite one another – everything is as you expected. You are reassured by repetition. But what is this? Now they are beginning a conversation! You are confused – can your memory really be so poor? Where you remembered the two of them as sitting in silence, now a dialogue is blossoming between them – inverted commas are springing up like flowers in a desert.

You've made some kind of mistake – you look through the book again. Now you see it. You realize that you have started reading another story in the collection, which only begins in the same manner as the first, but then strikes off in a wholly different direction. What a curious idea!

Night. The pen approaching the paper – firmly now, without hesitation. Letters written with the confidence of inevitable doom.

The new story begins, as before, with a train – who knows where it is heading? There are all the usual shudders and rattles, and the inexplicable sounds of a journey by rail – all of this, the author presents to you in exactly the same manner as before. The various rhythms and cadences of metal against greased metal, of interior fittings come loose, of swinging objects hanging freely from the luggage racks. Sleeves of discarded jackets waving forlornly as if in farewell to loved ones left behind, and baggage straps rocking with the steady metre of clock pendula.

All of this is quite familiar; it is all the same as when you were reading earlier. And you watch once more as the two characters find themselves sitting opposite one another. But now you have reached the point where the story diverges from the other version. Now the two of them have begun a conversation.

The girl is engrossed in her paperback. Perhaps you should say something to her. Far easier, though, to carry on reading your book, and imagine how things might be. She probably doesn't want to be disturbed from her reading anyway. When she takes a break, perhaps. You could ask her if it's a good book. Sometimes, while you're both reading, it feels as if she's catching a quick look at you whenever she turns a page.

Night. Dismal night. The pen being brought down onto the paper. Onto the final piece of paper.

You felt your knee bump against the girl's leg, beneath the table. Only a momentary touch. You were going to say sorry, but she hasn't looked up from her book. You're finding it hard to maintain your interest in the story; the distractions of the journey are intruding on your concentration. The book is only something to make you look occupied, while you study the face and body of the one who is sitting opposite you. You flick through the pages, and find another tale, about a man who sees a woman on a bus and immediately falls in love with her. The bus is just pulling away from the stop as the man walks past. He sees the girl sitting near the back – she looks up and he feels he must speak to her. He tries to get on the bus before it picks up speed but the doors are already closing and the bus goes away with the beautiful girl looking round over her shoulder. So he remembers the number of the bus and every day for a month he rides this route as often as he can – his job as a cafe waiter permitting – but he never sees her. Then one night who should walk into the cafe where he works but the girl – alone – and she goes and sits in a corner and brings out a little book – like a diary – and she starts writing in it. And he is on his way to take her order when another waiter called Luigi – whom he hates – beats him to it and fetches her a vermouth and chats to her a little before he goes to serve another customer. And although he is desperate to catch her eye she only writes in the little notebook or occasionally stares out into space and he thinks she looks somehow sad 'like a nightingale which has lost its song'.

Now what's this? Another woman has come along the passageway of the carriage, and she's eyeing the second empty seat which is facing you. She sits down – now there are two women for you to look at. The first is foreign looking – small and dark, almost boyish; this second one is less pretty, but she has a cool elegance which interests you. But now that there are two of them, you know that you won't be able to get anywhere with either. If you start a conversation with one, the other will only be an intruder.

Already you've missed your chance, Duncan. If you had spoken to that girl soon enough she would have told you her name was Giovanna – that she's from Cremona, in Italy (where the violins come from). And when the other woman came along she'd have seen you both talking and sat somewhere else so as not to interrupt, or be disturbed by you. You'd have found out all about this girl – you'd both have got on so well together. You'd have talked all the way to Leeds (or at least, she would). And you'd have offered her a place to stay tonight, since it's a nuisance looking for hotels – she would have agreed readily. Charles and Joanna would be there, but still it would all have worked out for the best in the end – not a good idea for her to sleep on the sofa, since she'd be in their way. A mattress on your bedroom floor instead. And then, and then, and then. But you've missed your chance – you could have been so happy together! Now you'll never know any more about her, what becomes of her. You'll never know any of it.

And the pen approaching the paper. The downward stroke, then the forlorn upward curve of a D. The swift creation of a word – Dear. Sitting alone, with the paper before him.

You're hardly paying attention to your book now – you're too busy watching the girl. You flick back to the strange story about two people on a train.

> The two of them have begun a conversation. She tells him that she is a writer, and finds train journeys – with their curious juxtaposition of motion and stasis – particularly conducive to the creative process. He takes this as a hint that she wants to be left to get on with some work.

A pity you won't be bringing Giovanna home with you. Charles would like her. And it would postpone the problem. How to deal with things now. He's sitting at the piano – drawing towards the end of the Goldberg Variations. He wonders what you'll have found in the files. He wonders what you know, and what you only suspect. He tries to decide what he'll tell you. He'll probably tell you nothing.

Now the ticket collector's coming. 'Ah. You've got a pink saver here. It's blue savers or standard fare today sir. I'm afraid you'll have to pay the difference.'

But you haven't got enough to give him. The two

women opposite eye you silently, as if you were some kind of criminal. You show him your identity card and he takes the details. Like some kind of criminal. Difficult to read again, now – you feel annoyed and irritated.

The girl wants to get on with some writing. The author describes how she reaches for her bag and rummages inside it – then cries out; her notebook is gone! She carries it with her wherever she goes, and now it's been stolen. She couldn't possibly have mislaid it – someone must have taken it. An admirer, or an autograph collector – perhaps another writer who is running short of ideas and has resorted to theft in lieu of inspiration.

Night. Alone – the paper before him. His last letter. Your father's last letter. The pallid light of the table lamp staining the wall. Cone of dismal yellow. How to find the words? The words – all those words he would like to leave behind.

Her notebook has gone – the opening chapters of a novel, gone without trace. Tears course down her cheeks as she tells how she shall have to begin all over again, her great story (though can you ever rediscover a story once it has been lost?). It was to have been a kind of detective story, set in a country which is under dictatorship. Two men are following each other, watching each other – perhaps they are friends, perhaps enemies. Difficult to tell, sometimes, whether someone is your friend or your enemy. Only fragments of their lives; brief glimpses from which to infer who they are, and what purpose there might be behind their actions. We see them meeting in a cafe, having a conversation – though through the thick window, we cannot hear their words. Or we see one of them going to meet a girl – following her through the streets until she reaches a door. He waits while she enters – he looks around, then goes inside.

Now it's reminding you again of the other story – subtle links you still don't understand. You look through the anthology again – a girl in a cafe, and a waiter who watches her while she writes. The stolen diary. Again, the idea of spying, of suspicion, of theft. You look at other pieces in the book – you skim through other tales; tales about letters which are surreptitiously removed from drawers, or about scraps of paper lost and found. Stories about a man pursuing a woman; or a woman, a man. About two men being followed by a third – the whole collection, though it seems to be a book of unrelated short stories, is really a single work; each piece is a fragment of something larger and perhaps unstated. A book about a theft, and a betrayal, and about secret observation.

It's like a revelation. You look up from the book, and you see those two women sitting opposite. You want to tell them how clever you are to have figured out what Galli is up to. But they're both buried in their own books.

A moment of silent self-congratulation – as if the author's achievement were somehow your own. And now, impatient as ever, you turn to the final story in the book.

28

The pen, rubbing its tip across the paper. A trail of blue ink – a single line – urgent and painful, and twisted, curled, sometimes angled, sometimes pulled back on itself. Back on itself – and broken only for the making of a dot, or a brief horizontal stroke. Or for the opening of an empty space. A single line, like a wire, bent into letters – letters of blue ink which have abandoned neatness – which have gone past caring about their own appearance. Dishevelled letters, broken symbols, and the forming of words – words which branch into meaning, or into several meanings, or into meaninglessness. Words which suggest a crime, or the idea of a crime – words which seem at first warm, but then grow colder. Words dead, even before their ink has dried.

Concerning the Library, we observe that its shelves extend in every direction beyond the limits of visibility. We suppose its contents to have been created by a single printing machine; each volume being of a uniform (and very great) length, and bound in brown leather. How many books does the Library contain? This is a simple calculation, involving only two pieces of data: the number of different symbols n (including the blank space) which the machine was capable of printing, and the maximum length l, in individual symbols, which a single book can contain. Then the extent of our Library is given by multiplying n by itself l-fold. The figure l, we have assessed from direct observation; a volume which is filled completely would take a lifetime to read in its entirety. Many tomes, however, contain a great number of blank pages. (The print is, of course, so fine as to require magnification, and the leaves are of extraordinary thinness and delicacy, so that great care is needed in turning them). As to the number n of possible symbols which can be printed, we assume this to be finite – in which case (if only one copy exists of each book) the Library itself must be of finite (though very great) extent. Some regard this as paradoxical, while for others, the notion that the shelves may continue without end is equally baffling. It is possible that there are other Libraries (that is to say, other Universes) consisting of works of greater length than can be housed in our own. However, if our Library is complete (in other words, if it consists of every possible permutation and combination of the allowed symbols within the allowed length), then we can be sure that it contains synopses, commentaries and abridged versions of everything which could not be included. (Many works in the Library will presumably take up several volumes – indeed, the entire Library could be regarded as a single huge opus).

She would have told you that her name is Giovanna – that she is from Cremona, in Italy. And she would have gone home with you tonight. So much easier than finding a hotel. She would have met Charles and Joanna. Then slept on a mattress on your bedroom floor. And then, and then.

Most of what we see is meaningless – page upon page of random symbols. (It is possible that the machine produced its text in some purely stochastic fashion; though a systematic procedure – such as working in strictly alphabetical order – would achieve the task in an equal length of time. In either case, the shelving seems to have been carried out without any method which we can discern). When, out of the incomprehensible jumble which fills most pages, a word or phrase suddenly emerges, then we know that this is simply a matter of chance, of good luck – a thought or observation, spewed out at random and then lost in the chaos of letters and symbols. Meaning is, after all, nothing more than a very special subset of something much greater – something without order or discipline.

The pen moving across the paper. Your father's last letter – his letter to Charles. The words placed together on the page – the erratic, uneven script as his hand moves nervously across the page.

What we know, however, is that if we spend long enough, and journey far enough, then we shall find books in which whole sentences make sense – or an entire page. What might they tell us? And rarest of all, if we searched for a sufficient period of time, there would be books whose entire contents would be meaningful – if not in our own language, then at least in one which is decipherable.

And next morning you would awaken, the two of you. Charles and Joanna already gone to work. The two of you alone.

Every book which has ever been written, or ever could be written by mortal hand, must be present in this great Library. Even the text which I am writing now is there already, somewhere – my every thought anticipated long ago by the unthinking machine. (Some books will seek to refute this assertion with vigour, while others will leave the matter undecided.)

You would already have shown her round the flat the previous evening – so interesting for her. Charles would have liked her. And she would have listened in awe while he tried to explain to her how light can be either a wave or a particle, depending on how you look at it. She would have told him that if only physics at school could have been so fascinating. Next morning, she would lie sleeping beside you. And you would leave her quietly, and go outside into the bright daylight.

To write, it would seem, is futile. It is better instead to explore – our own journeys through the Library are slow, and yield little. But we can suppose that there are others somewhere – in a region of which we know nothing – who will by now have discovered how to build craft capable of transporting them more quickly along the light-years of shelves (they will have discovered a book telling them how to do this). And among these people there will no longer be any need for writers; instead there will only be book explorers – fearless individuals who will go out on hazardous voyages in search of the book which will make them famous.

And what impulse would it be, when she awakens alone in the flat – morning sunshine streaming through the windows; what strange desire would lead her, while you went out briefly, to get up, and go into the little room which Charles King calls his study? And you would come back – you would open the front door quietly, and you would enter the flat once more, a pint of milk in your hand. And then you would see that the door of Charles's study is open. What unknown motive might have led her inside, to stare uncomprehendingly at the desk, with its litter of papers – sheets covered with meaningless formulae and symbols? And what impulse might have led her to open the drawer – what perverse kind of admiration for the unknown could fuel such an intrusion? The drawer, in the privacy of his study. And if you should come into the flat and see the door ajar, and if you should go inside – go into the study – then what scene of horror would be revealed to you?

And what is writing then, except a kind of theft? Theft from the library of ideas which the machine has provided us with. The Library which contains every possible book. Encyclopaedias of arcane knowledge, or of fallacy. Histories real and imagined, of lands which may never have existed, and not only tales of their past, but of all their futures also. Dictionaries

and grammars of languages living, dead, or as yet un-
coined.

So that my story, concerning the figure (or were
they figures?) whom I have pursued through this
labyrinth of shelves – the story of my observations,
my suspicions, my attempts to unravel the meaning behind their actions – this is a story which requires
no further elucidation. It would be a redundant tale –
a mere copying of that story which has already been
bound, somewhere, between covers of brown leather.
And if my story has (as I suspect is quite possible)
merely been stolen from the work of some other
writer, then I need not feel too guilty over this, since
he in his turn must surely have been pre-empted by
the infallible comprehensiveness of the Library; a
collection which houses the story – with all its beginnings, middles and resolutions – in every conceivable
form, style, manner and language.

The tales I have written are no more than shadows
– attempts to understand the vocabulary of events
which my observations have revealed; events which
I cannot understand, and which may perhaps have
no meaning, and yet which seem to come together
into some kind of pattern, or hierarchy of patterns;
events which suggest the possibility of a crime, or
the idea of another's guilt. Events which indicate
that not only do I observe, but I am myself observed.

Pointless, though, to write any more. What I seek
now is that volume (which, perhaps, they also seek –
the ones whom I pursue) – the book which will
contain all that I have seen, and written, and will
suggest perhaps some answer, or at least explain the
impossibility of such a fortunate conclusion.

She would have found what you have never searched for,
Duncan. She would be holding – like a sleepwalker, uncom-
prehending – the letter which your father wrote. The letter

which Charles has never destroyed. The letter which has lain in his drawer for years, like a sleeping monster. And which lies there still.

29

Dear Charles,

Already I am dead. If you are reading this, then it must be so. How strange it feels, to be writing to you as a dead man! My thoughts, feelings — my guilt — all of these seem so real to me, yet I know that as you read these words they are nothing more than abstractions for you to try and imagine; the thoughts of a man now dead, and his feelings, and his guilt.

It's so easy, when you're alone, to let ideas run riot — when they're your only companion, then you find they have a habit of taking on a life over which you have no control; you thought the ideas in your head were your slaves — your pets. But you find that they have a malicious will of their own, and a very special way of teasing and provoking you. Now, all of this must be over for me — thank God. Now at least, I must have found some kind of peace.

This is my last confession, Charles. I've no right to ask any favours, but for the sake of Anne and Duncan I beg you not to say a word of this to anyone.

I was the one who betrayed you. I planted the drugs in your flat. It was the time when I came round — the last time I saw you. What a terrible way to say goodbye! I went to the bathroom, and while I was out of your sight I put the packet under the carpet, just as they had told me to.

They made me do it, Charles — please believe me, I had no choice. They said it was only to 'warn' you; that they wouldn't take any more action — they only wanted to show you what they could do. But Anne told me on the phone what's been happening. I've ruined you. My own friend — the dearest friend in the world. I can't tell you how sick I feel — how much I loathe myself.

I did have a second interview with Mays — it was just after the weekend when we went out with Anne and Jenny (I was so wrong to make you suspect her!). I already knew that Mays had found out about Flood — but I didn't know how, or whether he had proof against either one of us. At first he was polite — almost friendly. but then he started asking about my family again and I knew he was threatening me — and toying with me. He asked me if I was interested in Greek poetry. You remember my translations in Flood? It was like when he asked me about Ganymede — as if he knew, but wasn't saying. He changed the subject — asked all kinds of things which seemed irrelevant. But still it was always questions, questions. He asked me about you, how well I knew you. If I trusted you. He tried to insinuate things. And then he showed me a little strip of paper. He held it up for me to read — my own writing. Does this mean anything to you, he said to me. I bent forward to read what was on the piece of paper — no use denying it was in my own hand. It said 'music, in a foreign language'. Part of the last line of one of the poems. The poems I signed 'Ganymede'. Now I knew that everything was lost.

He said they found it when they searched my office. Someone pulled a book off the shelf and the piece of paper was inside, like a bookmark. And then Mays turned the strip over for me to see — on the other side it said FLO 343592. Now it all made sense to me — it must have been the scrap which I tore from my notes when I took down your number. Almost the first time we played music together, and we talked about Flood. I took out a sheet I'd been using while working on a draft of the poem — I turned it over to the blank side, and wrote your number at the bottom. When I tore off the edge, I caught the last line on the other side. Later, I put it in a book and forgot about it. But it finally caught me.

He had your phone number with FLO written beside it, and he had a line of poetry. It seemed obscure, but harmless. Mays was obviously very proud of the stroke of luck which he chose to regard as inspiration. Just as a check, he started looking through the files, to see if FLO could refer to anything. And he found a copy of Flood — nothing to do with Jenny; it had been there for five years. All he had to do was read through it until he saw that poem. Then he read the articles, and he realized he was on to something. All that stuff about Cecil Grieve, and legalizing homo-sexuality.

He wanted to know what you had to do with it — I made up God knows how many excuses. There was nothing to implicate you except the number. But he still seemed to think that you were behind it all. He asked me if I was homosexual — I said no. Then he asked if you were. He said one of us had to have written that article — this was the thing he was getting so worked up about. Mays has got a very clear view on morality. That article — do you remember? The one I didn't want you to write.

The more I denied things, the worse it was making it for you. So I told him that I wrote it — that, and everything else. Flood was entirely my own idea, my own work. I had tried to get you to write something for it, but you refused. Of course, I could no longer deny my homosexuality. But by now I wasn't ashamed of anything any more — I had crossed some kind of frontier; each admission made the next one easier — almost pleasurable. I was proud to be confessing even to things of which I was wholly innocent. I knew that I was saving you — but also, in a way I can't describe, I felt then as if I was saving myself. And then at last when I was finished, I told Mays he could do whatever the hell he liked with me.

But he still wasn't convinced. He told me that Section Five had approved me for the book commission, and they didn't want the police to make waves. Mays said that for the moment he couldn't touch me. He called me all sorts of things. And then he got a policeman to rough me up. I thought at the time that something might be broken, but they're very expert at these things. Mays said that as far as he was concerned I was living on borrowed time — that once I'd finished the book he'd make sure I'd never work again. And he said that if I was to stand any chance then I'd have to return the favour they'd done me. They put me under a lot of pressure, Charles.

They said that you needed to be taught a lesson — as a warning. They wanted me to plant drugs in your flat. I refused of course — told them they could send me to jail for as long as they liked, but to leave you alone since you'd done nothing wrong. Mays still suspected you, though. He wanted something he could incriminate you with, just so as to keep you in check.

There'd be no charges, but you'd get the message. And if I didn't do it? Mays thought a bit. 'Lots of busy roads around here,' he said. 'It'd be a shame if little Duncan fell under a car.'

Maybe it was all idle threats, Charles, I don't know. But in the end I was weak. I gave in to them. I wish they'd killed me on the spot instead – but Duncan and Anne, I had to protect them. Wouldn't you have done the same?

Even when they gave me the drugs, I still held out for a week. Made excuses – avoided you. Mays was getting impatient. More threats – I thought I was going crazy. They said it was only to teach you a lesson.

So I betrayed you. And I fled to Scotland like a coward, with my notes for this damned book. A book that has been paid for with your job – your career. And who knows what else? I haven't exactly been in the best psychological state for writing – all I've managed to produce is a lot of rubbish. For three weeks, I've sat every day at the typewriter and watched the letters and words appear before me, but I feel like a mindless machine. And now that I've got the news from Anne – now that I know just what it is I've done to you, I can't go on any longer. This is the end for me, Charles. There's no other way.

I know how I'll do it – plenty of time here, alone, to think these things through. It'll all look like an accident – I know the right place for it. It'll be dark, I'll stop nearby – check that the road is clear. I don't want any witnesses. Take a deep breath, then drive full speed towards the bend; the road veering sharply to the right. I steer left. Then through the barrier, down that long hill. It'll be quick. Easier than I deserve. And everything will go flying through the air – all that there is of this book I hate so much, that's destroyed so much. All those typewritten sheets of nonsense falling out of the car and blowing away in the wind (I hope to God they don't find any of it). And the car will go tumbling down, bouncing. If I still know what's going on, I'll be happy. I'll be thinking of you, Charles.

And that's the last thing I want to confess; that I love you, and always have done. I wish only that the world could have been a different place – that the sort of love which I feel could be as easy and guiltless as yours, with all those women you have. I hope one day you'll find someone you can be content with. You were my great love, Charles — the one that everyone is supposed to have once in their life. And if anyone was ever to write our story, I hope it wouldn't be about intrigue and betrayal. I would want it to be a romance. A comedy.

I've no right to say any of this — especially after what I've done to you. But already I'm dead. Already I'm flying, floating. Take care of Anne and Duncan. Tell them nothing. I know what they both mean to you. Duncan is your own son — I've always known it, and it only made me love him more. Our child, yours and mine. And though I love Anne very much, I'm sure it's better for her that I should go. She can find herself a real husband now. Who knows, perhaps you two might make things up between you. It would make me happy.

One day Duncan will want to know about me — about what happened. I can't expect you to suffer the dishonour of defending me. But please try to forgive me. In my heart, I feel that everything I did, in the end, was out of love. I am a victim as much as you. Tell Duncan how much I loved him. I hope he grows up to be like you.

Goodbye.

Robert.

30

She was asking me (as was usual at such moments) what I was thinking about – so that I quickly had to think of some suitable reply. I told her I was thinking 'nothing'.

And that was the night when the novel first entered my imagination. Though not *this* novel – for I see already that I have failed in my attempt to unravel on paper the ideas which seemed so clear when they lived only in my mind. What I have written so far is nothing more than a series of first steps which one day might lead me to rediscover the book which had its conception that night. So easy, once you start putting things down, to get led off into new stories – stories you had no intention of writing. The lines I have spun up to now do little more than orbit around the real story. My task has still barely begun.

I told Eleonora I was thinking 'nothing', then went to the bathroom – its floor cold beneath my bare feet – and something prompted the memory of that girl whom I had briefly met ten years earlier. I had hardly thought of her since – what could have brought her once more to mind? I stood naked on the cold floor, in the dim half-light, and I found myself thinking of two people – Duncan and Giovanna, meeting on a train. For the next ten years, they would continue to grow in my imagination – a secret process, which I would never dare to confess. Yet even now, now that I am alone with my sorrows and I am free to languish in my fantasies, still I find that I am unable to write their story. If only I can get it right, that first scene, then surely everything else will follow. Still I cling to this hope.

That chance meeting – sitting on a train, on my way to visit Eleonora. On my way to that Turkish rug where our bodies had first come together. Reading a book by Alfredo Galli. And then that girl came into my compartment and sat opposite me. We began a conversation – she asked what had brought me to live in Italy, and I told her how I had sought asylum and was now earning a living teaching English. So like my first meeting with Eleonora! And yet this time things were crucially altered – where before I had been fascinated by coldness, now I saw something utterly alive. And it was a life which would be forever closed to me. I told her about the home I had left in England – my mother who was now all alone, since my father had died six years earlier (and my sister hardly visited). And how callous it had been of me to leave her so. No, the girl said, you mustn't feel like that – she even reached out her hand and placed it on my knee. But I'm sure now that by making my sudden flight into exile I hastened my mother's death. What ever would my father have thought of such behaviour?

Just as well, that I didn't think of him when I was standing on the cold bathroom floor. Just as well that I didn't think then, as so often I have done, of all the many ways in which I failed him – otherwise those two characters could never have walked unannounced into my imagination. Or might it have been better if I had thought of him, and thereby barred entry to the ones whose story I seem destined forever to go on redrafting?

But as the days and weeks passed, and Duncan and Giovanna began to emerge more clearly in my mind, I found that other memories were being drawn into the strange process of accretion which was taking place, and which has borne its first fruit in the pages I have now filled. As Galli said in his final work – the *Essay Against Literature* – 'If the writer is one who holds a mirror to the world, then it is necessarily a broken mirror; reflecting the points of reality, but distorting the distances which separate them.' The story I have been trying to set down is indeed a kind of broken mirror. And now, as I think back on what I have written during my journeys each day between Cremona and Milan, I can see how things have been altered and distorted. And I ask myself whether the mirror can be made true once more. Flat and true.

She drew her hand back from my knee. Still we were sitting close opposite one another in the compartment. She asked me more about my parents — what they were like; and we talked about childhood, and its weird perspective which can cast shadows across an entire life. Surprising, how easy it can be, sometimes, to talk to a complete stranger.

I told her about my father; a proud, cool man. He was in the police. He had no education, but still he was able to rise eventually to the rank of Inspector. He often said I had inherited my talent for science from his own enquiring mind. And what a mind! While I was still a young child, his unerring ability to discover any misbehaviour which I might have committed made me think that he must have the capacity to read my thoughts. In his work, I have no doubt, he was equally efficient. If only I could have been as good at science.

I reminisced with her about the times when he would take me to watch trains near our house, and he would silently hold my hand while I waved at the passing engines. Perhaps he would use the time to mull over a difficult case. And we agreed that one's parents are always the people one knows least in the world. Only in retrospect can we try to piece together the lives which they must have led — only by reflecting on our own fears and anxieties can we speculate about the ones which they must have felt.

Standing in the cold bathroom, the memory of the girl's face, and the sound of her voice, came back to me — still fresh — across a space of years. I went back to bed, fell asleep beside my wife, but already the act of mental infidelity was well under way. And in the weeks which followed, I began to learn more about the fictional characters who had sprung to life in my head.

An evening some time later; I went to the bathroom before going to bed (why should it always be the bathroom? Perhaps because it was only here that I could enjoy true privacy), and as I pulled up my flies, I thought of that time as a child when I got myself caught in the zip — my father had joked that if things had gone wrong I might have come out Jewish. And I remembered wondering then, with the pure clear logic of childhood, if this was the sort of error which had been committed by those boys who now wore a yellow star, and were being sent away. Such a vivid memory, no matter how many times it recurs. And standing there, I saw again in my mind the stolen notebook, and the car – white, in my imagination – and the memory of all those many ways in which I had tried to explain it. So that when I went to bed and lay silent and subdued beside Eleonora and she asked me what I was thinking, and I told her as usual 'nothing', in fact my mind was filled with troubling thoughts. And I could see now how the story should begin – not with two people on a train, but rather with an image; the image of a car hitting a barrier, and tumbling down a hillside.

Sitting in the compartment, the girl's knees close to mine as we sat opposite one another. She told me about a boy she thought she was in love with, though she wasn't sure – how can you ever be sure about a thing like love? To be sure usually means being deluded. She told me about her own childhood, and how she would secretly put on her mother's make-up and clothes – walking around the bedroom in high-heels which were ten sizes too big for her. And I told her how I used to play at being a policeman, like my father.

Once, when I was very young, I went into his room while he was out. I opened the drawer of his desk, and saw a small notebook – his policeman's pocket-book. Perhaps he shouldn't have kept such a thing at home – though I now realize it wasn't the usual regulation notebook (I have checked these things thoroughly). I saw it lying in the drawer. What impulse led me to take it out, to open it, and to study without comprehension the writing which my father had entered in it? I should have put it back – and yet I didn't. I kept it – stole it. This little record of other people's guilt became a symbol of my own. Secretly, I used it in my games. If I had been

236

discovered, who knows what punishment I might have deserved?

I could only have been four or five – I can't remember if it was before the Liberation or after. Certainly, I was too young to be able to understand anything which was written in it. I only wanted to have a prop with which to emulate my father; to have a notebook just like his. Even so, I knew that I must never be found out. I hid the book away, in a box deep in a drawer in the spare room. And I forgot about it.

I forgot about it for more than twenty years. I had grown up, left home and gone to university. Now I was doing research in theoretical physics. My father had died, and mother decided to sell the house and move to a smaller place. She asked me to come and help put things in order. It was strange, returning to the scene of my childhood – I had been back many times, of course, but now that I was going through cupboards and boxes, rediscovering the past, it brought me once more into close contact with the lost years. And in the spare room, still buried at the bottom of the drawer, I found the notebook I had hidden long ago. It had lain there all that time, dormant. I opened it again, and looked at the coloured swirls I had pencilled across its pages with my childish hand. But now, with the eye of an adult, I could read the text which my father had written – the police notes which I had stolen. Perhaps he got into a lot of trouble for losing his notebook. Or else he covered his error by simply taking a new one and making things up from memory or imagination. Perhaps my actions set a man free – and perhaps I caused another to be condemned.

I still have the book – why is it that I can never bring myself to destroy it? I still feel the ache of guilt which its theft caused in my stomach. And yet it is all I have left of him. Five years after I rediscovered it, when I was preparing to make my one-way journey to Italy, it was the only thing I took as a memento. And the notes it contains have continued to intrigue me – the barest details of a case concerning two men. Who they were, I do not know. Nor can I be certain whether the events took place during the Occupation or under the Communist regime. The book is not of the standard form used by the police during either period (though my father's service covered both) – it seems that it may have been connected with something covert; something which lay outside the normal scope of police work. The pages I tore out during my childhood games might have supplied an answer. Or perhaps, now that the files are open, I shall find the courage to go back to England to try and learn the full story.

The briefest of notes – each man followed; sometimes they meet, sometimes it appears that one of them himself is following the other. Two suspicious souls themselves suspected. Did my theft enable them to walk free? Or was the evidence against them irrelevant? My father – although he later reached the rank of Inspector – would at that time only have been a constable. He could have been little more than an unseen player, blind to the greater meaning and implication of whatever it was he was doing. And so in those notes, there is no sense of purpose; no sense of who might be the criminal, or what the offence. There are only observations, dry and objective like the records of a scientist engaged in some experiment. Observations written in the neat, evenly sloping letters of my father; letters which form words with no meaning and yet which seem to imply a crime, or the idea of a crime. And as I stood in the house of my parents – in the house of my childhood – with the little book I had rediscovered, and I read beneath the childish spirals with which I had embellished his words – followed those neatly formed letters – I was reminded of my own crime, of my own act of theft; I was reminded that this forgotten episode was itself part of my own guilt – and no guilt is greater than that of a child. I felt again the lump of fear in my throat; I heard again my father's stern voice – and I saw him watching his suspects; a different kind of figure now. Now he too was being watched, his memory was being judged, assessed. What small part might he have played in the story he was describing? And exactly whose story was it?

Two men, one or both of whom may have been involved in subversion; one or both of whom may have been a collaborator, or an informer. We see one of them, observed in a cafe, writing something - a diary perhaps. Or the other going to meet a girl – we follow the two of them through the streets, to a door which they enter. And there is a car which, my father notes, 'will be dealt with'.

An unofficial, covert operation. Not a standard piece of police work. I have tried out many theories – a simple surveillance job for a friend who suspected his wife, or a piece of unpaid overtime by a young constable keen on promotion. Harmless possibilities. Or he may have been part of one of those secret sections within the police. He may have been involved in activities which were less than honourable. So painful for me to contemplate it, and yet these fears have lingered with me ever since I stood in my mother's house and deciphered the words which had lain hidden for so long. Fears which stayed with me when I went to Italy a few years later – the book still in my possession (such a risk to take it!) – no hope then of finding an answer. Fears which I never dared discuss with Eleonora throughout twenty years of marriage. And yet I confessed everything to that girl whose name I never learned.

If my father's notes were written during the Occupation, then might the suspects have been with the Resistance? In which case, my father may have crossed the boundary which branded some sections of the police as active collaborators, rather than the passive ones who were immediately pardoned and rehabilitated. My father would have committed the ultimate act of treachery. But if it was during the Communist regime, would this make things any better? The difference between being a hero or a traitor is simply a matter of being on the right side at the right time.

Perhaps, now that the records are being opened, all will become clear. And then they will prove that my father was only doing his job, only following orders. That although he was strong, he could also be weak – and this was the side of him which I might have loved if I had ever been able to see it. And when I see how wrong I have been, I shall beg forgiveness from his memory.

I was standing in the bathroom, brushing my teeth. Stories were flowing together in my mind, like rivers merging; Duncan and Giovanna, and a car – a white car, crashing through a barrier. And memories of the days I spent in England doing research; memories of the things I had left behind; people I had abandoned and betrayed. And I thought of Galli's words, at the end of his *Essay Against Literature*: 'The writer can never escape from reality, no matter how hard he might try; for the flight from the world is a flight into one's soul, and this is a land in which there can be no excuses, no justifications. To write is to be forever the slave of one's talents, and the prisoner of one's failings.'

I got into bed beside Eleonora's sleek body, and though I told her I was thinking 'nothing', my mind was filled with troublesome thoughts. Now I had it; the story of Duncan and Giovanna, and of the car crash which killed his father – his father who was an historian, a scientist experimenting with the past; a man who was supposed to contribute to the rewriting of history but who would make a stand, and who would die because of it. And a friend who was a successful physicist – who was everything that I was not. Everything that my father might have liked me to be. And a third man, called Mays – a name which reflected the labyrinthine nature of Possibility. For ten years, their story would grow in my mind. During the day I would be able to forget about it, but it was in the nights that it would return – this secret obsession. I would follow them, these elusive figures, through the shelves of Galli's great Library, in search of the solution which I would one day write.

Was I mad, to spend so much time thinking about these fantasies – these illusions? Sometimes I was reminded of those poor deranged souls – when I was a physicist in

England – who were constantly writing to us with their crazy theories of the Universe. Is a writer any better than one of those misled people? Is a writer not merely someone who has lost touch with reality, and become submerged in his own fictions?

But the process was irresistible – I realized that I was little more than a receptacle for thoughts which were moving under their own volition. I knew now what Galli meant in his last essay; the last thing he wrote before he ended his own life with the same careless ease he had applied to so many of his stories. I was a prisoner of my past, and a slave of my own fears.

And yet I wrote nothing. And while I waited, history took its incredible course. Britain at last became free again – we watched it all happen on the television. And when Eleanora passed away some months afterwards, there was no longer anything left for me here in Italy – no excuse for me not to return to the homeland I had fled.

And once more the story had changed – Duncan was supposed to have been an exile, who meets Giovanna on the way to Milan. But now the story would be set in Britain – now Duncan would be able to consult the files to find out everything. I had the final ingredient. Now all I needed was to take some blank paper onto the train with me one morning.

But it's so easy, to get led off track. I wanted to write about two people who meet on a train, who fall in love, whose lives become forever entwined – and in the end they aren't even talking to each other! I wanted to write about a young man in search of the truth about his father – a heroic father, prepared to die for his ideals. But it all went wrong. All because of Flood.

There was never supposed to be any Flood; it simply appeared, while I was writing – and it stole my story away from me, made everything go astray. Strange, how the smallest things can have such great consequences. Which is more terrible – to die for something you should never have done, or to die for something which ought never even to have existed?

So now I shall have to begin again – please, forget everything you have read. This is all little more than a rough draft. As for the real book, the one which has haunted me for so long – well, I realize my search will have to continue. But I know it's still out there somewhere.

Remember Galli's universal Library – an idea which was genuinely his, though the tales which Duncan read were all of course my own invention. I hope that Galli would not have been too offended by my act of plagiarism – after all, as he himself said, all writing is theft. The novel I am looking for sits there on a shelf somewhere – who knows where? And so do all the other versions which I shall write in the course of my search, and all those which I shall never write. And somewhere too, in that vast collection, there is the story of my life – the book which tells what is to happen to me; whether I shall ever succeed in my task, or whether I am to be a sort of Flying Dutchman, forever circling around the book I dream of without being able to come to port. And not only the story of my life, but of all the other lives I could have had – a story in which I never left England, or one in which I married that girl I met long ago. There will be all the possible stories of your life also (many, but nevertheless a finite number). And in some of those stories, you will never read my words, while in others you will not only read them, but our lives will become linked in ways more interesting than the arid relationship of author and reader. And there will be stories too, in some corner of our cosmic Library, in which it is not I who have written this book, but you – and I am merely one of your readers.

I am nearly home. Now I sit, with my work dismantled on my lap like a defective pocket watch. When I try to put it all together again, will it go any better? Tomorrow morning, I shall catch my train once more, with a fresh sheaf of paper under my arm.

Nearly two years since Eleonora left me. It's easier now – the memories less painful. And I find myself allowing certain thoughts which not long ago seemed abhorrent. I am no longer afraid of the idea that I might meet someone and remarry.

And let me now confess to you my final dream – a dream which has lain in my heart for years, though I did not dare admit it. A dream which comes vividly to me again as it has come so many times before, but which now, at last, I need no longer resist.

I am sitting on the train, when a girl gets on and takes the seat opposite me. I look up, and I see that it is she – the one whom I lost so long ago. In my mind, I see her just as she was then, still fresh and young, while I have withered with the years. At first she doesn't recognize me, but gradually she realizes who I am, and she tells me with joy that she too has been longing for me, waiting for me. It's as if our two souls have been buried in ash, petrified and unable to touch each other – but now free at last to come together. Such a fond embrace, after all those years we have spent apart!

And now we are man and wife – young again with happiness, and lying together in our bed. We have just made the most joyous act of love, and she asks me what I am thinking about. When I tell her, she does not frown or look annoyed. Nor does she express any displeasure when I say that I am thinking of the beginning of a novel – a novel which one day I shall write, about two people who meet on a train. She asks me excitedly to tell her about it, and so I say that it all begins with an image; the image of a motor car crashing through a barrier, and tumbling down a hill. And she tells me that she would like to hear the rest of it.

About the Author

Andrew Crumey was born in Glasgow in 1961. He read theoretical physics and mathematics at St Andrews University and Imperial College, before doing post doctoral research at Leeds University on nonlinear dynamics. He now lives in Newcastle upon Tyne.

Music, In A Foreign Language is his first novel.